The *Pottery Addict's*
Project Journal

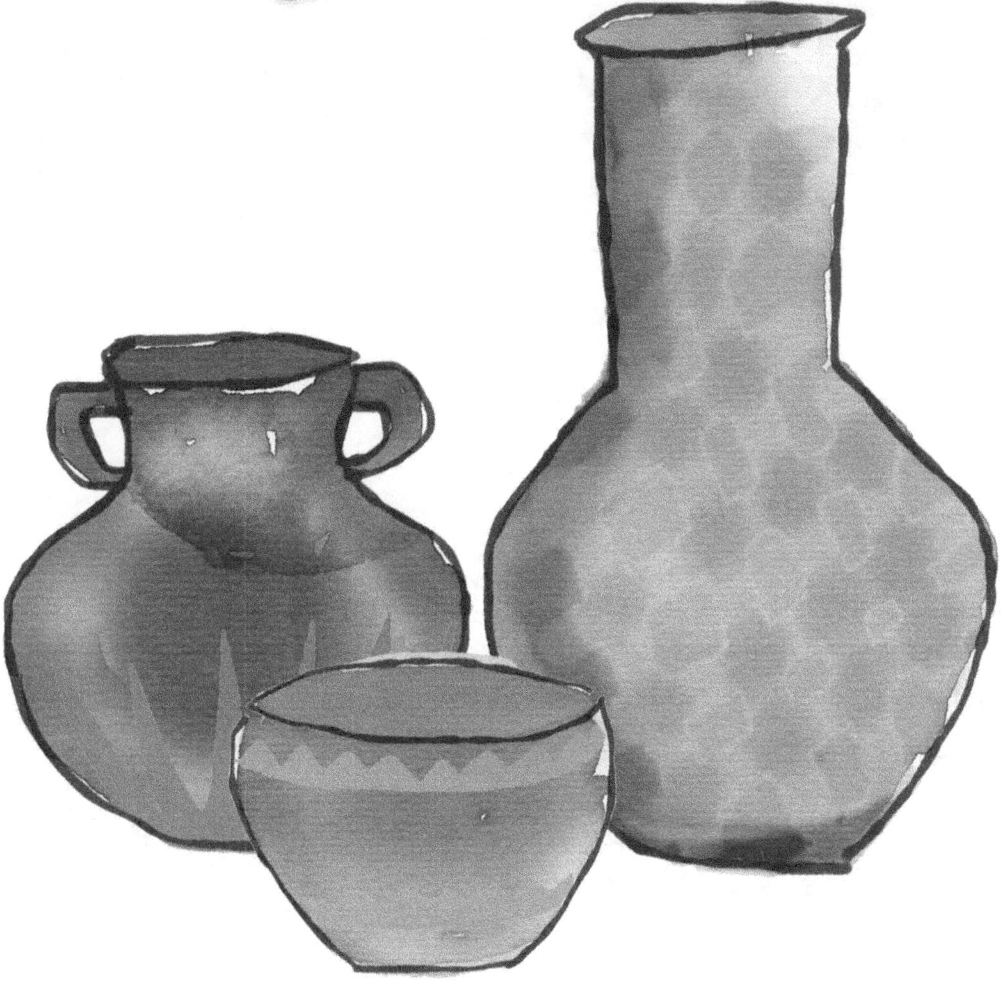

Nola Lee Kelsey

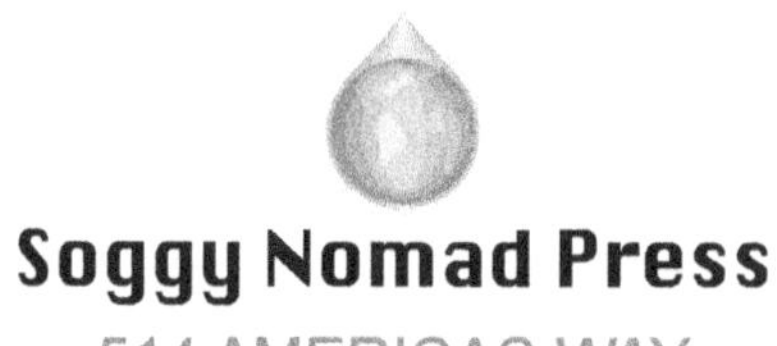

Soggy Nomad Press

514 AMERICAS WAY
STE: 17697
BOX ELDER, SD 57719

ISBN: 978-1-957532-00-4

Cover design by Nola Lee Kelsey

"To practice any art, no matter how well or badly, is a way to make your soul grow. So do it."

-- Kurt Vonnegut

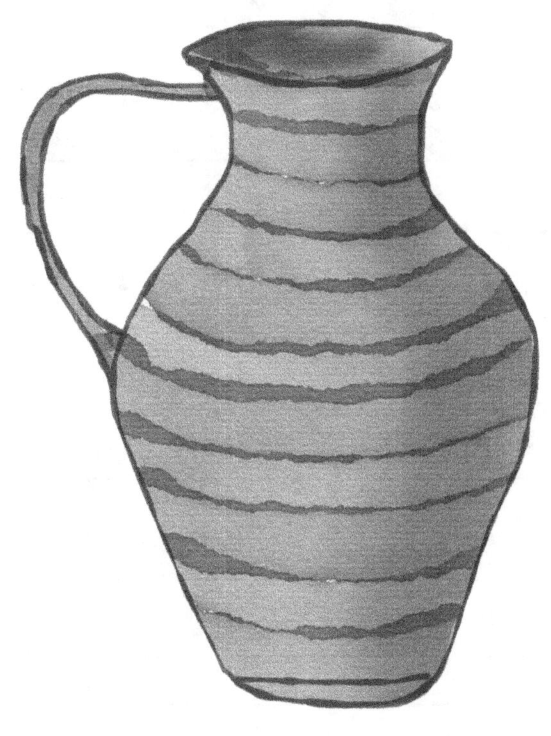

PROJECT: **DATE:**

IMAGE or SKETCH

DIMENSIONS: WEIGHT:

CLAY

TYPE:		COLOR:	SOURCE:	
ADDITIVE(S):				RESULTS RATING:

FORMING TECHNIQUE(S):

DECORATING TECHNIQUES & TOOLS:

DRYING TIME/NOTES:

BISQUE FIRING   DATE

KILN TYPE:	PROGRAM OR FIRING METHOD:	CONE:
PREHEAT/HOLD/COOL FIRING TIME/TEMP(S):		TOTAL TIME:
STAINS/SPRAYS/COMBUSTIBLES:		

Glaze(s)

BRAND:	COLOR/TRANSPARENCY/CHARACTERISTICS		
APPLICATION METHOD(S):		COATS/LAYER:	FOOD SAFE? **YES NO**

BRAND:	COLOR/TRANSPARENCY/CHARACTERISTICS		
APPLICATION METHOD(S):		COATS/LAYER:	FOOD SAFE? **YES NO**

BRAND:	COLOR/TRANSPARENCY/CHARACTERISTICS		
APPLICATION METHOD(S):		COATS/LAYER:	FOOD SAFE? **YES NO**

BRAND:	COLOR/TRANSPARENCY/CHARACTERISTICS		
APPLICATION METHOD(S):		COATS/LAYER:	FOOD SAFE? **YES NO**

BRAND:	COLOR/TRANSPARENCY/CHARACTERISTICS		
APPLICATION METHOD(S):		COATS/LAYER:	FOOD SAFE? **YES NO**

GLAZE FIRING 1   DATE

KILN TYPE:	PROGRAM OR FIRING METHOD:	CONE:
PREHEAT/HOLD/COOL FIRING TIME/TEMP(S):		TOTAL TIME:

GLAZE/LUSTER FIRING   DATE

KILN TYPE:	PROGRAM OR FIRING METHOD:	CONE:
PREHEAT/HOLD/COOL FIRING TIME/TEMP(S):		TOTAL TIME:

NOTES:

____

____

____

____

____

SALES RECORD

SALE LOCATION:	ESTIMATED VALUE/LISTING PRICE:
SALE DATE:	TRANSACTION DETAILS:	FINAL PRICE:

PROJECT: **DATE:**

IMAGE or SKETCH

DIMENSIONS: WEIGHT:

CLAY

TYPE:		COLOR:	SOURCE:	
ADDITIVE(S):				RESULTS RATING:

FORMING TECHNIQUE(S):

DECORATING TECHNIQUES & TOOLS:

DRYING TIME/NOTES:

BISQUE FIRING   DATE

KILN TYPE:	PROGRAM OR FIRING METHOD:		CONE:
PREHEAT/HOLD/COOL FIRING TIME/TEMP(S):			TOTAL TIME:
STAINS/SPRAYS/COMBUSTIBLES:			

Glaze(s)

BRAND:	COLOR/TRANSPARENCY/CHARACTERISTICS		
APPLICATION METHOD(S):		COATS/LAYER:	FOOD SAFE? **YES NO**

BRAND:	COLOR/TRANSPARENCY/CHARACTERISTICS		
APPLICATION METHOD(S):		COATS/LAYER:	FOOD SAFE? **YES NO**

BRAND:	COLOR/TRANSPARENCY/CHARACTERISTICS		
APPLICATION METHOD(S):		COATS/LAYER:	FOOD SAFE? **YES NO**

BRAND:	COLOR/TRANSPARENCY/CHARACTERISTICS		
APPLICATION METHOD(S):		COATS/LAYER:	FOOD SAFE? **YES NO**

BRAND:	COLOR/TRANSPARENCY/CHARACTERISTICS		
APPLICATION METHOD(S):		COATS/LAYER:	FOOD SAFE? **YES NO**

GLAZE FIRING 1   DATE

KILN TYPE:	PROGRAM OR FIRING METHOD:	CONE:
PREHEAT/HOLD/COOL FIRING TIME/TEMP(S):		TOTAL TIME:

GLAZE/LUSTER FIRING   DATE

KILN TYPE:	PROGRAM OR FIRING METHOD:	CONE:
PREHEAT/HOLD/COOL FIRING TIME/TEMP(S):		TOTAL TIME:

NOTES:

____

____

____

____

____

SALES RECORD

SALE LOCATION:	ESTIMATED VALUE/LISTING PRICE:	
SALE DATE:	TRANSACTION DETAILS:	FINAL PRICE:

PROJECT: **DATE:**

IMAGE or SKETCH

DIMENSIONS: **WEIGHT:**

CLAY

TYPE:	COLOR:	SOURCE:
ADDITIVE(S):		RESULTS RATING:

FORMING TECHNIQUE(S):

DECORATING TECHNIQUES & TOOLS:

DRYING TIME/NOTES:

BISQUE FIRING   DATE

KILN TYPE:	PROGRAM OR FIRING METHOD:	CONE:
PREHEAT/HOLD/COOL FIRING TIME/TEMP(S):		TOTAL TIME:
STAINS/SPRAYS/COMBUSTIBLES:		

Glaze(s)

BRAND:	COLOR/TRANSPARENCY/CHARACTERISTICS		
APPLICATION METHOD(S):		COATS/LAYER:	FOOD SAFE? **YES NO**

BRAND:	COLOR/TRANSPARENCY/CHARACTERISTICS		
APPLICATION METHOD(S):		COATS/LAYER:	FOOD SAFE? **YES NO**

BRAND:	COLOR/TRANSPARENCY/CHARACTERISTICS		
APPLICATION METHOD(S):		COATS/LAYER:	FOOD SAFE? **YES NO**

BRAND:	COLOR/TRANSPARENCY/CHARACTERISTICS		
APPLICATION METHOD(S):		COATS/LAYER:	FOOD SAFE? **YES NO**

BRAND:	COLOR/TRANSPARENCY/CHARACTERISTICS		
APPLICATION METHOD(S):		COATS/LAYER:	FOOD SAFE? **YES NO**

GLAZE FIRING 1   DATE

KILN TYPE:	PROGRAM OR FIRING METHOD:	CONE:
PREHEAT/HOLD/COOL FIRING TIME/TEMP(S):		TOTAL TIME:

GLAZE/LUSTER FIRING   DATE

KILN TYPE:	PROGRAM OR FIRING METHOD:	CONE:
PREHEAT/HOLD/COOL FIRING TIME/TEMP(S):		TOTAL TIME:

NOTES:

____

____

____

____

____

SALES RECORD

SALE LOCATION:	ESTIMATED VALUE/LISTING PRICE:
SALE DATE:	TRANSACTION DETAILS:	FINAL PRICE:

PROJECT:

DATE:

IMAGE or SKETCH

DIMENSIONS:

WEIGHT:

CLAY

TYPE:	COLOR:	SOURCE:

ADDITIVE(S):	RESULTS RATING:

FORMING TECHNIQUE(S):

DECORATING TECHNIQUES & TOOLS:

DRYING TIME/NOTES:

BISQUE FIRING   DATE

KILN TYPE:	PROGRAM OR FIRING METHOD:	CONE:

PREHEAT/HOLD/COOL FIRING TIME/TEMP(S):	TOTAL TIME:

STAINS/SPRAYS/COMBUSTIBLES:

Glaze(s)

BRAND:	COLOR/TRANSPARENCY/CHARACTERISTICS		
APPLICATION METHOD(S):		COATS/LAYER:	FOOD SAFE? **YES NO**

BRAND:	COLOR/TRANSPARENCY/CHARACTERISTICS		
APPLICATION METHOD(S):		COATS/LAYER:	FOOD SAFE? **YES NO**

BRAND:	COLOR/TRANSPARENCY/CHARACTERISTICS		
APPLICATION METHOD(S):		COATS/LAYER:	FOOD SAFE? **YES NO**

BRAND:	COLOR/TRANSPARENCY/CHARACTERISTICS		
APPLICATION METHOD(S):		COATS/LAYER:	FOOD SAFE? **YES NO**

BRAND:	COLOR/TRANSPARENCY/CHARACTERISTICS		
APPLICATION METHOD(S):		COATS/LAYER:	FOOD SAFE? **YES NO**

GLAZE FIRING 1   DATE

KILN TYPE:	PROGRAM OR FIRING METHOD:	CONE:
PREHEAT/HOLD/COOL FIRING TIME/TEMP(S):		TOTAL TIME:

GLAZE/LUSTER FIRING   DATE

KILN TYPE:	PROGRAM OR FIRING METHOD:	CONE:
PREHEAT/HOLD/COOL FIRING TIME/TEMP(S):		TOTAL TIME:

NOTES:

____

____

____

____

____

SALES RECORD

SALE LOCATION:	ESTIMATED VALUE/LISTING PRICE:
SALE DATE: TRANSACTION DETAILS:	FINAL PRICE:

PROJECT: DATE:

IMAGE or SKETCH

DIMENSIONS: WEIGHT:

CLAY

TYPE:		COLOR:	SOURCE:	
ADDITIVE(S):				RESULTS RATING:

FORMING TECHNIQUE(S):

DECORATING TECHNIQUES & TOOLS:

DRYING TIME/NOTES:

BISQUE FIRING   DATE

KILN TYPE:	PROGRAM OR FIRING METHOD:	CONE:
PREHEAT/HOLD/COOL FIRING TIME/TEMP(S):		TOTAL TIME:
STAINS/SPRAYS/COMBUSTIBLES:		

Glaze(s)

BRAND:	COLOR/TRANSPARENCY/CHARACTERISTICS		
APPLICATION METHOD(S):		COATS/LAYER:	FOOD SAFE? **YES NO**

BRAND:	COLOR/TRANSPARENCY/CHARACTERISTICS		
APPLICATION METHOD(S):		COATS/LAYER:	FOOD SAFE? **YES NO**

BRAND:	COLOR/TRANSPARENCY/CHARACTERISTICS		
APPLICATION METHOD(S):		COATS/LAYER:	FOOD SAFE? **YES NO**

BRAND:	COLOR/TRANSPARENCY/CHARACTERISTICS		
APPLICATION METHOD(S):		COATS/LAYER:	FOOD SAFE? **YES NO**

BRAND:	COLOR/TRANSPARENCY/CHARACTERISTICS		
APPLICATION METHOD(S):		COATS/LAYER:	FOOD SAFE? **YES NO**

GLAZE FIRING 1   DATE

KILN TYPE:	PROGRAM OR FIRING METHOD:	CONE:
PREHEAT/HOLD/COOL FIRING TIME/TEMP(S):		TOTAL TIME:

GLAZE/LUSTER FIRING   DATE

KILN TYPE:	PROGRAM OR FIRING METHOD:	CONE:
PREHEAT/HOLD/COOL FIRING TIME/TEMP(S):		TOTAL TIME:

NOTES:

____

____

____

____

____

SALES RECORD

SALE LOCATION:	ESTIMATED VALUE/LISTING PRICE:
SALE DATE:	TRANSACTION DETAILS:	FINAL PRICE:

PROJECT: **DATE:**

DIMENSIONS: WEIGHT:

CLAY

TYPE:	COLOR:	SOURCE:
ADDITIVE(S):		RESULTS RATING:

FORMING TECHNIQUE(S):

DECORATING TECHNIQUES & TOOLS:

DRYING TIME/NOTES:

BISQUE FIRING   DATE

KILN TYPE:	PROGRAM OR FIRING METHOD:	CONE:
PREHEAT/HOLD/COOL FIRING TIME/TEMP(S):		TOTAL TIME:
STAINS/SPRAYS/COMBUSTIBLES:		

Glaze(s)

BRAND:	COLOR/TRANSPARENCY/CHARACTERISTICS		
APPLICATION METHOD(S):		COATS/LAYER:	FOOD SAFE? **YES NO**

BRAND:	COLOR/TRANSPARENCY/CHARACTERISTICS		
APPLICATION METHOD(S):		COATS/LAYER:	FOOD SAFE? **YES NO**

BRAND:	COLOR/TRANSPARENCY/CHARACTERISTICS		
APPLICATION METHOD(S):		COATS/LAYER:	FOOD SAFE? **YES NO**

BRAND:	COLOR/TRANSPARENCY/CHARACTERISTICS		
APPLICATION METHOD(S):		COATS/LAYER:	FOOD SAFE? **YES NO**

BRAND:	COLOR/TRANSPARENCY/CHARACTERISTICS		
APPLICATION METHOD(S):		COATS/LAYER:	FOOD SAFE? **YES NO**

GLAZE FIRING 1   DATE

KILN TYPE:	PROGRAM OR FIRING METHOD:	CONE:
PREHEAT/HOLD/COOL FIRING TIME/TEMP(S):		TOTAL TIME:

GLAZE/LUSTER FIRING   DATE

KILN TYPE:	PROGRAM OR FIRING METHOD:	CONE:
PREHEAT/HOLD/COOL FIRING TIME/TEMP(S):		TOTAL TIME:

NOTES:

____

____

____

____

____

SALES RECORD

SALE LOCATION:	ESTIMATED VALUE/LISTING PRICE:
SALE DATE:	TRANSACTION DETAILS:	FINAL PRICE:

PROJECT: **DATE:**

IMAGE or SKETCH

DIMENSIONS: **WEIGHT:**

CLAY

TYPE:	COLOR:	SOURCE:
ADDITIVE(S):		RESULTS RATING:

FORMING TECHNIQUE(S):

DECORATING TECHNIQUES & TOOLS:

DRYING TIME/NOTES:

BISQUE FIRING   DATE

KILN TYPE:	PROGRAM OR FIRING METHOD:	CONE:
PREHEAT/HOLD/COOL FIRING TIME/TEMP(S):		TOTAL TIME:
STAINS/SPRAYS/COMBUSTIBLES:		

Glaze(s)

BRAND:	COLOR/TRANSPARENCY/CHARACTERISTICS		
APPLICATION METHOD(S):		COATS/LAYER:	FOOD SAFE? **YES NO**

BRAND:	COLOR/TRANSPARENCY/CHARACTERISTICS		
APPLICATION METHOD(S):		COATS/LAYER:	FOOD SAFE? **YES NO**

BRAND:	COLOR/TRANSPARENCY/CHARACTERISTICS		
APPLICATION METHOD(S):		COATS/LAYER:	FOOD SAFE? **YES NO**

BRAND:	COLOR/TRANSPARENCY/CHARACTERISTICS		
APPLICATION METHOD(S):		COATS/LAYER:	FOOD SAFE? **YES NO**

BRAND:	COLOR/TRANSPARENCY/CHARACTERISTICS		
APPLICATION METHOD(S):		COATS/LAYER:	FOOD SAFE? **YES NO**

GLAZE FIRING 1   DATE

KILN TYPE:	PROGRAM OR FIRING METHOD:	CONE:
PREHEAT/HOLD/COOL FIRING TIME/TEMP(S):		TOTAL TIME:

GLAZE/LUSTER FIRING   DATE

KILN TYPE:	PROGRAM OR FIRING METHOD:	CONE:
PREHEAT/HOLD/COOL FIRING TIME/TEMP(S):		TOTAL TIME:

NOTES:

____

____

____

____

____

SALES RECORD

SALE LOCATION:	ESTIMATED VALUE/LISTING PRICE:
SALE DATE:	TRANSACTION DETAILS:	FINAL PRICE:

PROJECT: **DATE:**

IMAGE or SKETCH

DIMENSIONS: WEIGHT:

CLAY

TYPE:	COLOR:	SOURCE:
ADDITIVE(S):		RESULTS RATING:

FORMING TECHNIQUE(S):

DECORATING TECHNIQUES & TOOLS:

DRYING TIME/NOTES:

BISQUE FIRING   DATE

KILN TYPE:	PROGRAM OR FIRING METHOD:	CONE:
PREHEAT/HOLD/COOL FIRING TIME/TEMP(S):		TOTAL TIME:
STAINS/SPRAYS/COMBUSTIBLES:		

Glaze(s)

BRAND:	COLOR/TRANSPARENCY/CHARACTERISTICS		
APPLICATION METHOD(S):		COATS/LAYER:	FOOD SAFE? **YES NO**

BRAND:	COLOR/TRANSPARENCY/CHARACTERISTICS		
APPLICATION METHOD(S):		COATS/LAYER:	FOOD SAFE? **YES NO**

BRAND:	COLOR/TRANSPARENCY/CHARACTERISTICS		
APPLICATION METHOD(S):		COATS/LAYER:	FOOD SAFE? **YES NO**

BRAND:	COLOR/TRANSPARENCY/CHARACTERISTICS		
APPLICATION METHOD(S):		COATS/LAYER:	FOOD SAFE? **YES NO**

BRAND:	COLOR/TRANSPARENCY/CHARACTERISTICS		
APPLICATION METHOD(S):		COATS/LAYER:	FOOD SAFE? **YES NO**

GLAZE FIRING 1   DATE

KILN TYPE:	PROGRAM OR FIRING METHOD:	CONE:
PREHEAT/HOLD/COOL FIRING TIME/TEMP(S):		TOTAL TIME:

GLAZE/LUSTER FIRING   DATE

KILN TYPE:	PROGRAM OR FIRING METHOD:	CONE:
PREHEAT/HOLD/COOL FIRING TIME/TEMP(S):		TOTAL TIME:

NOTES:

____

____

____

____

____

SALES RECORD

SALE LOCATION:	ESTIMATED VALUE/LISTING PRICE:	
SALE DATE:	TRANSACTION DETAILS:	FINAL PRICE:

PROJECT: **DATE:**

IMAGE or SKETCH

DIMENSIONS: **WEIGHT:**

CLAY

TYPE:	COLOR:	SOURCE:
ADDITIVE(S):		RESULTS RATING:

FORMING TECHNIQUE(S):

DECORATING TECHNIQUES & TOOLS:

DRYING TIME/NOTES:

BISQUE FIRING   DATE

KILN TYPE:	PROGRAM OR FIRING METHOD:	CONE:
PREHEAT/HOLD/COOL FIRING TIME/TEMP(S):		TOTAL TIME:
STAINS/SPRAYS/COMBUSTIBLES:		

Glaze(s)

BRAND:	COLOR/TRANSPARENCY/CHARACTERISTICS		
APPLICATION METHOD(S):		COATS/LAYER:	FOOD SAFE? **YES NO**

BRAND:	COLOR/TRANSPARENCY/CHARACTERISTICS		
APPLICATION METHOD(S):		COATS/LAYER:	FOOD SAFE? **YES NO**

BRAND:	COLOR/TRANSPARENCY/CHARACTERISTICS		
APPLICATION METHOD(S):		COATS/LAYER:	FOOD SAFE? **YES NO**

BRAND:	COLOR/TRANSPARENCY/CHARACTERISTICS		
APPLICATION METHOD(S):		COATS/LAYER:	FOOD SAFE? **YES NO**

BRAND:	COLOR/TRANSPARENCY/CHARACTERISTICS		
APPLICATION METHOD(S):		COATS/LAYER:	FOOD SAFE? **YES NO**

GLAZE FIRING 1   DATE

KILN TYPE:	PROGRAM OR FIRING METHOD:	CONE:
PREHEAT/HOLD/COOL FIRING TIME/TEMP(S):		TOTAL TIME:

GLAZE/LUSTER FIRING   DATE

KILN TYPE:	PROGRAM OR FIRING METHOD:	CONE:
PREHEAT/HOLD/COOL FIRING TIME/TEMP(S):		TOTAL TIME:

NOTES:

____

____

____

____

____

SALES RECORD

SALE LOCATION:	ESTIMATED VALUE/LISTING PRICE:
SALE DATE:	TRANSACTION DETAILS:	FINAL PRICE:

PROJECT: **DATE:**

IMAGE or SKETCH

DIMENSIONS: WEIGHT:

CLAY

TYPE:	COLOR:	SOURCE:

ADDITIVE(S):	RESULTS RATING:

FORMING TECHNIQUE(S):

DECORATING TECHNIQUES & TOOLS:

DRYING TIME/NOTES:

BISQUE FIRING   DATE

KILN TYPE:	PROGRAM OR FIRING METHOD:	CONE:

PREHEAT/HOLD/COOL FIRING TIME/TEMP(S):	TOTAL TIME:

STAINS/SPRAYS/COMBUSTIBLES:

Glaze(s)

BRAND:	COLOR/TRANSPARENCY/CHARACTERISTICS		
APPLICATION METHOD(S):		COATS/LAYER:	FOOD SAFE? **YES NO**

BRAND:	COLOR/TRANSPARENCY/CHARACTERISTICS		
APPLICATION METHOD(S):		COATS/LAYER:	FOOD SAFE? **YES NO**

BRAND:	COLOR/TRANSPARENCY/CHARACTERISTICS		
APPLICATION METHOD(S):		COATS/LAYER:	FOOD SAFE? **YES NO**

BRAND:	COLOR/TRANSPARENCY/CHARACTERISTICS		
APPLICATION METHOD(S):		COATS/LAYER:	FOOD SAFE? **YES NO**

BRAND:	COLOR/TRANSPARENCY/CHARACTERISTICS		
APPLICATION METHOD(S):		COATS/LAYER:	FOOD SAFE? **YES NO**

GLAZE FIRING 1   DATE

KILN TYPE:	PROGRAM OR FIRING METHOD:	CONE:
PREHEAT/HOLD/COOL FIRING TIME/TEMP(S):		TOTAL TIME:

GLAZE/LUSTER FIRING   DATE

KILN TYPE:	PROGRAM OR FIRING METHOD:	CONE:
PREHEAT/HOLD/COOL FIRING TIME/TEMP(S):		TOTAL TIME:

NOTES:

____

____

____

____

____

SALES RECORD

SALE LOCATION:	ESTIMATED VALUE/LISTING PRICE:
SALE DATE: TRANSACTION DETAILS:	FINAL PRICE:

PROJECT: ___________________________   **DATE:** ___________________________

IMAGE or SKETCH

DIMENSIONS: ___________________________   WEIGHT: ___________________________

CLAY

TYPE:	COLOR:	SOURCE:

ADDITIVE(S):	RESULTS RATING:

FORMING TECHNIQUE(S):

____

____

____

DECORATING TECHNIQUES & TOOLS:

____

____

____

DRYING TIME/NOTES:

____

____

BISQUE FIRING   DATE

KILN TYPE:	PROGRAM OR FIRING METHOD:	CONE:

PREHEAT/HOLD/COOL FIRING TIME/TEMP(S):	TOTAL TIME:

STAINS/SPRAYS/COMBUSTIBLES:

Glaze(s)

BRAND:	COLOR/TRANSPARENCY/CHARACTERISTICS		
APPLICATION METHOD(S):		COATS/LAYER:	FOOD SAFE? **YES NO**

BRAND:	COLOR/TRANSPARENCY/CHARACTERISTICS		
APPLICATION METHOD(S):		COATS/LAYER:	FOOD SAFE? **YES NO**

BRAND:	COLOR/TRANSPARENCY/CHARACTERISTICS		
APPLICATION METHOD(S):		COATS/LAYER:	FOOD SAFE? **YES NO**

BRAND:	COLOR/TRANSPARENCY/CHARACTERISTICS		
APPLICATION METHOD(S):		COATS/LAYER:	FOOD SAFE? **YES NO**

BRAND:	COLOR/TRANSPARENCY/CHARACTERISTICS		
APPLICATION METHOD(S):		COATS/LAYER:	FOOD SAFE? **YES NO**

GLAZE FIRING 1   DATE

KILN TYPE:	PROGRAM OR FIRING METHOD:	CONE:
PREHEAT/HOLD/COOL FIRING TIME/TEMP(S):		TOTAL TIME:

GLAZE/LUSTER FIRING   DATE

KILN TYPE:	PROGRAM OR FIRING METHOD:	CONE:
PREHEAT/HOLD/COOL FIRING TIME/TEMP(S):		TOTAL TIME:

NOTES:

____

____

____

____

____

SALES RECORD

SALE LOCATION:	ESTIMATED VALUE/LISTING PRICE:	
SALE DATE:	TRANSACTION DETAILS:	FINAL PRICE:

PROJECT:

DATE:

IMAGE or SKETCH

DIMENSIONS:

WEIGHT:

CLAY

TYPE:	COLOR:	SOURCE:

ADDITIVE(S):	RESULTS RATING:

FORMING TECHNIQUE(S):

DECORATING TECHNIQUES & TOOLS:

DRYING TIME/NOTES:

BISQUE FIRING   DATE

KILN TYPE:	PROGRAM OR FIRING METHOD:	CONE:

PREHEAT/HOLD/COOL FIRING TIME/TEMP(S):	TOTAL TIME:

STAINS/SPRAYS/COMBUSTIBLES:

Glaze(s)

<table>
<tr><td>BRAND:</td><td colspan="3">COLOR/TRANSPARENCY/CHARACTERISTICS</td></tr>
<tr><td>APPLICATION METHOD(S):</td><td>COATS/LAYER:</td><td colspan="2">FOOD SAFE?
YES NO</td></tr>
<tr><td>BRAND:</td><td colspan="3">COLOR/TRANSPARENCY/CHARACTERISTICS</td></tr>
<tr><td>APPLICATION METHOD(S):</td><td>COATS/LAYER:</td><td colspan="2">FOOD SAFE?
YES NO</td></tr>
<tr><td>BRAND:</td><td colspan="3">COLOR/TRANSPARENCY/CHARACTERISTICS</td></tr>
<tr><td>APPLICATION METHOD(S):</td><td>COATS/LAYER:</td><td colspan="2">FOOD SAFE?
YES NO</td></tr>
<tr><td>BRAND:</td><td colspan="3">COLOR/TRANSPARENCY/CHARACTERISTICS</td></tr>
<tr><td>APPLICATION METHOD(S):</td><td>COATS/LAYER:</td><td colspan="2">FOOD SAFE?
YES NO</td></tr>
<tr><td>BRAND:</td><td colspan="3">COLOR/TRANSPARENCY/CHARACTERISTICS</td></tr>
<tr><td>APPLICATION METHOD(S):</td><td>COATS/LAYER:</td><td colspan="2">FOOD SAFE?
YES NO</td></tr>
</table>

GLAZE FIRING 1   DATE

KILN TYPE:	PROGRAM OR FIRING METHOD:	CONE:
PREHEAT/HOLD/COOL FIRING TIME/TEMP(S):		TOTAL TIME:

GLAZE/LUSTER FIRING   DATE

KILN TYPE:	PROGRAM OR FIRING METHOD:	CONE:
PREHEAT/HOLD/COOL FIRING TIME/TEMP(S):		TOTAL TIME:

NOTES:

____

____

____

____

SALES RECORD

SALE LOCATION:	ESTIMATED VALUE/LISTING PRICE:
SALE DATE: TRANSACTION DETAILS:	FINAL PRICE:

PROJECT: **DATE:**

IMAGE or SKETCH

DIMENSIONS: **WEIGHT:**

CLAY

TYPE:	COLOR:	SOURCE:
ADDITIVE(S):		RESULTS RATING:

FORMING TECHNIQUE(S):

DECORATING TECHNIQUES & TOOLS:

DRYING TIME/NOTES:

BISQUE FIRING   DATE

KILN TYPE:	PROGRAM OR FIRING METHOD:	CONE:
PREHEAT/HOLD/COOL FIRING TIME/TEMP(S):		TOTAL TIME:
STAINS/SPRAYS/COMBUSTIBLES:		

Glaze(s)

<table>
<tr><td>BRAND:</td><td colspan="2">COLOR/TRANSPARENCY/CHARACTERISTICS</td><td></td></tr>
<tr><td>APPLICATION METHOD(S):</td><td>COATS/LAYER:</td><td>FOOD SAFE?</td><td>YES NO</td></tr>
<tr><td>BRAND:</td><td colspan="2">COLOR/TRANSPARENCY/CHARACTERISTICS</td><td></td></tr>
<tr><td>APPLICATION METHOD(S):</td><td>COATS/LAYER:</td><td>FOOD SAFE?</td><td>YES NO</td></tr>
<tr><td>BRAND:</td><td colspan="2">COLOR/TRANSPARENCY/CHARACTERISTICS</td><td></td></tr>
<tr><td>APPLICATION METHOD(S):</td><td>COATS/LAYER:</td><td>FOOD SAFE?</td><td>YES NO</td></tr>
<tr><td>BRAND:</td><td colspan="2">COLOR/TRANSPARENCY/CHARACTERISTICS</td><td></td></tr>
<tr><td>APPLICATION METHOD(S):</td><td>COATS/LAYER:</td><td>FOOD SAFE?</td><td>YES NO</td></tr>
<tr><td>BRAND:</td><td colspan="2">COLOR/TRANSPARENCY/CHARACTERISTICS</td><td></td></tr>
<tr><td>APPLICATION METHOD(S):</td><td>COATS/LAYER:</td><td>FOOD SAFE?</td><td>YES NO</td></tr>
</table>

GLAZE FIRING 1   DATE

KILN TYPE:	PROGRAM OR FIRING METHOD:	CONE:
PREHEAT/HOLD/COOL FIRING TIME/TEMP(S):		TOTAL TIME:

GLAZE/LUSTER FIRING   DATE

KILN TYPE:	PROGRAM OR FIRING METHOD:	CONE:
PREHEAT/HOLD/COOL FIRING TIME/TEMP(S):		TOTAL TIME:

NOTES:

____

____

____

____

____

SALES RECORD

SALE LOCATION:	ESTIMATED VALUE/LISTING PRICE:
SALE DATE:	TRANSACTION DETAILS:	FINAL PRICE:

PROJECT: **DATE:**

IMAGE or SKETCH

DIMENSIONS: WEIGHT:

CLAY

TYPE:		COLOR:	SOURCE:	
ADDITIVE(S):				RESULTS RATING:

FORMING TECHNIQUE(S):

DECORATING TECHNIQUES & TOOLS:

DRYING TIME/NOTES:

BISQUE FIRING   DATE

KILN TYPE:	PROGRAM OR FIRING METHOD:	CONE:
PREHEAT/HOLD/COOL FIRING TIME/TEMP(S):		TOTAL TIME:
STAINS/SPRAYS/COMBUSTIBLES:		

Glaze(s)

BRAND:	COLOR/TRANSPARENCY/CHARACTERISTICS		
APPLICATION METHOD(S):		COATS/LAYER:	FOOD SAFE? **YES NO**

BRAND:	COLOR/TRANSPARENCY/CHARACTERISTICS		
APPLICATION METHOD(S):		COATS/LAYER:	FOOD SAFE? **YES NO**

BRAND:	COLOR/TRANSPARENCY/CHARACTERISTICS		
APPLICATION METHOD(S):		COATS/LAYER:	FOOD SAFE? **YES NO**

BRAND:	COLOR/TRANSPARENCY/CHARACTERISTICS		
APPLICATION METHOD(S):		COATS/LAYER:	FOOD SAFE? **YES NO**

BRAND:	COLOR/TRANSPARENCY/CHARACTERISTICS		
APPLICATION METHOD(S):		COATS/LAYER:	FOOD SAFE? **YES NO**

GLAZE FIRING 1   DATE

KILN TYPE:	PROGRAM OR FIRING METHOD:	CONE:
PREHEAT/HOLD/COOL FIRING TIME/TEMP(S):		TOTAL TIME:

GLAZE/LUSTER FIRING   DATE

KILN TYPE:	PROGRAM OR FIRING METHOD:	CONE:
PREHEAT/HOLD/COOL FIRING TIME/TEMP(S):		TOTAL TIME:

NOTES:

____

____

____

____

____

SALES RECORD

SALE LOCATION:	ESTIMATED VALUE/LISTING PRICE:	
SALE DATE:	TRANSACTION DETAILS:	FINAL PRICE:

PROJECT: **DATE:**

IMAGE or SKETCH

DIMENSIONS: WEIGHT:

CLAY

TYPE:		COLOR:	SOURCE:	
ADDITIVE(S):				RESULTS RATING:

FORMING TECHNIQUE(S):

DECORATING TECHNIQUES & TOOLS:

DRYING TIME/NOTES:

BISQUE FIRING   DATE

KILN TYPE:	PROGRAM OR FIRING METHOD:	CONE:
PREHEAT/HOLD/COOL FIRING TIME/TEMP(S):		TOTAL TIME:
STAINS/SPRAYS/COMBUSTIBLES:		

Glaze(s)

BRAND:	COLOR/TRANSPARENCY/CHARACTERISTICS		
APPLICATION METHOD(S):		COATS/LAYER:	FOOD SAFE? **YES NO**

BRAND:	COLOR/TRANSPARENCY/CHARACTERISTICS		
APPLICATION METHOD(S):		COATS/LAYER:	FOOD SAFE? **YES NO**

BRAND:	COLOR/TRANSPARENCY/CHARACTERISTICS		
APPLICATION METHOD(S):		COATS/LAYER:	FOOD SAFE? **YES NO**

BRAND:	COLOR/TRANSPARENCY/CHARACTERISTICS		
APPLICATION METHOD(S):		COATS/LAYER:	FOOD SAFE? **YES NO**

BRAND:	COLOR/TRANSPARENCY/CHARACTERISTICS		
APPLICATION METHOD(S):		COATS/LAYER:	FOOD SAFE? **YES NO**

GLAZE FIRING 1   DATE

KILN TYPE:	PROGRAM OR FIRING METHOD:	CONE:
PREHEAT/HOLD/COOL FIRING TIME/TEMP(S):		TOTAL TIME:

GLAZE/LUSTER FIRING   DATE

KILN TYPE:	PROGRAM OR FIRING METHOD:	CONE:
PREHEAT/HOLD/COOL FIRING TIME/TEMP(S):		TOTAL TIME:

NOTES:

____

____

____

____

SALES RECORD

SALE LOCATION:		ESTIMATED VALUE/LISTING PRICE:
SALE DATE:	TRANSACTION DETAILS:	FINAL PRICE:

PROJECT: **DATE:**

IMAGE or SKETCH

DIMENSIONS: WEIGHT:

CLAY

TYPE:		COLOR:	SOURCE:
ADDITIVE(S):			RESULTS RATING:

FORMING TECHNIQUE(S):

DECORATING TECHNIQUES & TOOLS:

DRYING TIME/NOTES:

BISQUE FIRING   DATE

KILN TYPE:	PROGRAM OR FIRING METHOD:	CONE:
PREHEAT/HOLD/COOL FIRING TIME/TEMP(S):		TOTAL TIME:
STAINS/SPRAYS/COMBUSTIBLES:		

Glaze(s)

<table>
<tr><td>BRAND:</td><td colspan="2">COLOR/TRANSPARENCY/CHARACTERISTICS</td><td></td></tr>
<tr><td>APPLICATION METHOD(S):</td><td></td><td>COATS/LAYER:</td><td>FOOD SAFE?
YES   NO</td></tr>
<tr><td>BRAND:</td><td colspan="2">COLOR/TRANSPARENCY/CHARACTERISTICS</td><td></td></tr>
<tr><td>APPLICATION METHOD(S):</td><td></td><td>COATS/LAYER:</td><td>FOOD SAFE?
YES   NO</td></tr>
<tr><td>BRAND:</td><td colspan="2">COLOR/TRANSPARENCY/CHARACTERISTICS</td><td></td></tr>
<tr><td>APPLICATION METHOD(S):</td><td></td><td>COATS/LAYER:</td><td>FOOD SAFE?
YES   NO</td></tr>
<tr><td>BRAND:</td><td colspan="2">COLOR/TRANSPARENCY/CHARACTERISTICS</td><td></td></tr>
<tr><td>APPLICATION METHOD(S):</td><td></td><td>COATS/LAYER:</td><td>FOOD SAFE?
YES   NO</td></tr>
<tr><td>BRAND:</td><td colspan="2">COLOR/TRANSPARENCY/CHARACTERISTICS</td><td></td></tr>
<tr><td>APPLICATION METHOD(S):</td><td></td><td>COATS/LAYER:</td><td>FOOD SAFE?
YES   NO</td></tr>
</table>

GLAZE FIRING 1   DATE

KILN TYPE:	PROGRAM OR FIRING METHOD:	CONE:
PREHEAT/HOLD/COOL FIRING TIME/TEMP(S):		TOTAL TIME:

GLAZE/LUSTER FIRING   DATE

KILN TYPE:	PROGRAM OR FIRING METHOD:	CONE:
PREHEAT/HOLD/COOL FIRING TIME/TEMP(S):		TOTAL TIME:

NOTES:

____

____

____

____

____

SALES RECORD

SALE LOCATION:	ESTIMATED VALUE/LISTING PRICE:
SALE DATE:	TRANSACTION DETAILS:	FINAL PRICE:

PROJECT: **DATE:**

IMAGE or SKETCH

DIMENSIONS: **WEIGHT:**

CLAY

TYPE:	COLOR:	SOURCE:
ADDITIVE(S):		RESULTS RATING:

FORMING TECHNIQUE(S):

DECORATING TECHNIQUES & TOOLS:

DRYING TIME/NOTES:

BISQUE FIRING   DATE

KILN TYPE:	PROGRAM OR FIRING METHOD:	CONE:
PREHEAT/HOLD/COOL FIRING TIME/TEMP(S):		TOTAL TIME:
STAINS/SPRAYS/COMBUSTIBLES:		

Glaze(s)

BRAND:	COLOR/TRANSPARENCY/CHARACTERISTICS		
APPLICATION METHOD(S):		COATS/LAYER:	FOOD SAFE? **YES NO**

BRAND:	COLOR/TRANSPARENCY/CHARACTERISTICS		
APPLICATION METHOD(S):		COATS/LAYER:	FOOD SAFE? **YES NO**

BRAND:	COLOR/TRANSPARENCY/CHARACTERISTICS		
APPLICATION METHOD(S):		COATS/LAYER:	FOOD SAFE? **YES NO**

BRAND:	COLOR/TRANSPARENCY/CHARACTERISTICS		
APPLICATION METHOD(S):		COATS/LAYER:	FOOD SAFE? **YES NO**

BRAND:	COLOR/TRANSPARENCY/CHARACTERISTICS		
APPLICATION METHOD(S):		COATS/LAYER:	FOOD SAFE? **YES NO**

GLAZE FIRING 1   DATE

KILN TYPE:	PROGRAM OR FIRING METHOD:	CONE:
PREHEAT/HOLD/COOL FIRING TIME/TEMP(S):		TOTAL TIME:

GLAZE/LUSTER FIRING   DATE

KILN TYPE:	PROGRAM OR FIRING METHOD:	CONE:
PREHEAT/HOLD/COOL FIRING TIME/TEMP(S):		TOTAL TIME:

NOTES:

____

____

____

____

____

SALES RECORD

SALE LOCATION:	ESTIMATED VALUE/LISTING PRICE:
SALE DATE:	TRANSACTION DETAILS:	FINAL PRICE:

PROJECT: ________________________________   **DATE:** ________________

IMAGE or SKETCH

DIMENSIONS: ________________________________   WEIGHT: ________________

CLAY

TYPE:	COLOR:	SOURCE:
ADDITIVE(S):		RESULTS RATING:

FORMING TECHNIQUE(S):

____

____

DECORATING TECHNIQUES & TOOLS:

____

____

DRYING TIME/NOTES:

____

BISQUE FIRING   DATE

KILN TYPE:	PROGRAM OR FIRING METHOD:	CONE:
PREHEAT/HOLD/COOL FIRING TIME/TEMP(S):		TOTAL TIME:
STAINS/SPRAYS/COMBUSTIBLES:		

Glaze(s)

BRAND:	COLOR/TRANSPARENCY/CHARACTERISTICS		
APPLICATION METHOD(S):		COATS/LAYER:	FOOD SAFE? **YES NO**

BRAND:	COLOR/TRANSPARENCY/CHARACTERISTICS		
APPLICATION METHOD(S):		COATS/LAYER:	FOOD SAFE? **YES NO**

BRAND:	COLOR/TRANSPARENCY/CHARACTERISTICS		
APPLICATION METHOD(S):		COATS/LAYER:	FOOD SAFE? **YES NO**

BRAND:	COLOR/TRANSPARENCY/CHARACTERISTICS		
APPLICATION METHOD(S):		COATS/LAYER:	FOOD SAFE? **YES NO**

BRAND:	COLOR/TRANSPARENCY/CHARACTERISTICS		
APPLICATION METHOD(S):		COATS/LAYER:	FOOD SAFE? **YES NO**

GLAZE FIRING 1   DATE

KILN TYPE:	PROGRAM OR FIRING METHOD:	CONE:
PREHEAT/HOLD/COOL FIRING TIME/TEMP(S):		TOTAL TIME:

GLAZE/LUSTER FIRING   DATE

KILN TYPE:	PROGRAM OR FIRING METHOD:	CONE:
PREHEAT/HOLD/COOL FIRING TIME/TEMP(S):		TOTAL TIME:

NOTES:

____

____

____

____

____

SALES RECORD

SALE LOCATION:	ESTIMATED VALUE/LISTING PRICE:
SALE DATE:	TRANSACTION DETAILS:	FINAL PRICE:

PROJECT: DATE:

IMAGE or SKETCH

DIMENSIONS: WEIGHT:

CLAY

TYPE:		COLOR:	SOURCE:
ADDITIVE(S):			RESULTS RATING:

FORMING TECHNIQUE(S):

DECORATING TECHNIQUES & TOOLS:

DRYING TIME/NOTES:

BISQUE FIRING   DATE

KILN TYPE:	PROGRAM OR FIRING METHOD:	CONE:
PREHEAT/HOLD/COOL FIRING TIME/TEMP(S):		TOTAL TIME:
STAINS/SPRAYS/COMBUSTIBLES:		

Glaze(s)

BRAND:	COLOR/TRANSPARENCY/CHARACTERISTICS		
APPLICATION METHOD(S):		COATS/LAYER:	FOOD SAFE? **YES NO**

BRAND:	COLOR/TRANSPARENCY/CHARACTERISTICS		
APPLICATION METHOD(S):		COATS/LAYER:	FOOD SAFE? **YES NO**

BRAND:	COLOR/TRANSPARENCY/CHARACTERISTICS		
APPLICATION METHOD(S):		COATS/LAYER:	FOOD SAFE? **YES NO**

BRAND:	COLOR/TRANSPARENCY/CHARACTERISTICS		
APPLICATION METHOD(S):		COATS/LAYER:	FOOD SAFE? **YES NO**

BRAND:	COLOR/TRANSPARENCY/CHARACTERISTICS		
APPLICATION METHOD(S):		COATS/LAYER:	FOOD SAFE? **YES NO**

GLAZE FIRING 1   DATE

KILN TYPE:	PROGRAM OR FIRING METHOD:	CONE:
PREHEAT/HOLD/COOL FIRING TIME/TEMP(S):		TOTAL TIME:

GLAZE/LUSTER FIRING   DATE

KILN TYPE:	PROGRAM OR FIRING METHOD:	CONE:
PREHEAT/HOLD/COOL FIRING TIME/TEMP(S):		TOTAL TIME:

NOTES:

____

____

____

____

____

SALES RECORD

SALE LOCATION:		ESTIMATED VALUE/LISTING PRICE:
SALE DATE:	TRANSACTION DETAILS:	FINAL PRICE:

PROJECT: **DATE:**

IMAGE or SKETCH

DIMENSIONS: WEIGHT:

CLAY

TYPE:	COLOR:	SOURCE:
ADDITIVE(S):		RESULTS RATING:

FORMING TECHNIQUE(S):

DECORATING TECHNIQUES & TOOLS:

DRYING TIME/NOTES:

BISQUE FIRING   DATE

KILN TYPE:	PROGRAM OR FIRING METHOD:	CONE:
PREHEAT/HOLD/COOL FIRING TIME/TEMP(S):		TOTAL TIME:
STAINS/SPRAYS/COMBUSTIBLES:		

Glaze(s)

BRAND:	COLOR/TRANSPARENCY/CHARACTERISTICS		
APPLICATION METHOD(S):		COATS/LAYER:	FOOD SAFE? **YES NO**

BRAND:	COLOR/TRANSPARENCY/CHARACTERISTICS		
APPLICATION METHOD(S):		COATS/LAYER:	FOOD SAFE? **YES NO**

BRAND:	COLOR/TRANSPARENCY/CHARACTERISTICS		
APPLICATION METHOD(S):		COATS/LAYER:	FOOD SAFE? **YES NO**

BRAND:	COLOR/TRANSPARENCY/CHARACTERISTICS		
APPLICATION METHOD(S):		COATS/LAYER:	FOOD SAFE? **YES NO**

BRAND:	COLOR/TRANSPARENCY/CHARACTERISTICS		
APPLICATION METHOD(S):		COATS/LAYER:	FOOD SAFE? **YES NO**

GLAZE FIRING 1   DATE

KILN TYPE:	PROGRAM OR FIRING METHOD:	CONE:
PREHEAT/HOLD/COOL FIRING TIME/TEMP(S):		TOTAL TIME:

GLAZE/LUSTER FIRING   DATE

KILN TYPE:	PROGRAM OR FIRING METHOD:	CONE:
PREHEAT/HOLD/COOL FIRING TIME/TEMP(S):		TOTAL TIME:

NOTES:

____

____

____

____

____

SALES RECORD

SALE LOCATION:	ESTIMATED VALUE/LISTING PRICE:
SALE DATE:	TRANSACTION DETAILS:	FINAL PRICE:

PROJECT: _______________________   **DATE:** _______________

IMAGE or SKETCH

DIMENSIONS: _______________________   WEIGHT: _______________

CLAY

TYPE:	COLOR:	SOURCE:
ADDITIVE(S):		RESULTS RATING:

FORMING TECHNIQUE(S):

____

____

____

DECORATING TECHNIQUES & TOOLS:

____

____

____

DRYING TIME/NOTES:

____

____

BISQUE FIRING   DATE

KILN TYPE:	PROGRAM OR FIRING METHOD:	CONE:
PREHEAT/HOLD/COOL FIRING TIME/TEMP(S):		TOTAL TIME:
STAINS/SPRAYS/COMBUSTIBLES:		

Glaze(s)

BRAND:	COLOR/TRANSPARENCY/CHARACTERISTICS		
APPLICATION METHOD(S):		COATS/LAYER:	FOOD SAFE? **YES NO**

BRAND:	COLOR/TRANSPARENCY/CHARACTERISTICS		
APPLICATION METHOD(S):		COATS/LAYER:	FOOD SAFE? **YES NO**

BRAND:	COLOR/TRANSPARENCY/CHARACTERISTICS		
APPLICATION METHOD(S):		COATS/LAYER:	FOOD SAFE? **YES NO**

BRAND:	COLOR/TRANSPARENCY/CHARACTERISTICS		
APPLICATION METHOD(S):		COATS/LAYER:	FOOD SAFE? **YES NO**

BRAND:	COLOR/TRANSPARENCY/CHARACTERISTICS		
APPLICATION METHOD(S):		COATS/LAYER:	FOOD SAFE? **YES NO**

GLAZE FIRING 1   DATE

KILN TYPE:	PROGRAM OR FIRING METHOD:	CONE:
PREHEAT/HOLD/COOL FIRING TIME/TEMP(S):		TOTAL TIME:

GLAZE/LUSTER FIRING   DATE

KILN TYPE:	PROGRAM OR FIRING METHOD:	CONE:
PREHEAT/HOLD/COOL FIRING TIME/TEMP(S):		TOTAL TIME:

NOTES:

____

____

____

____

____

SALES RECORD

SALE LOCATION:	ESTIMATED VALUE/LISTING PRICE:
SALE DATE:	TRANSACTION DETAILS:	FINAL PRICE:

PROJECT:

DATE:

IMAGE or SKETCH

DIMENSIONS:

WEIGHT:

CLAY

TYPE:	COLOR:	SOURCE:

ADDITIVE(S):	RESULTS RATING:

FORMING TECHNIQUE(S):

DECORATING TECHNIQUES & TOOLS:

DRYING TIME/NOTES:

BISQUE FIRING   DATE

KILN TYPE:	PROGRAM OR FIRING METHOD:	CONE:

PREHEAT/HOLD/COOL FIRING TIME/TEMP(S):	TOTAL TIME:

STAINS/SPRAYS/COMBUSTIBLES:

Glaze(s)

BRAND:	COLOR/TRANSPARENCY/CHARACTERISTICS		
APPLICATION METHOD(S):		COATS/LAYER:	FOOD SAFE? **YES NO**

BRAND:	COLOR/TRANSPARENCY/CHARACTERISTICS		
APPLICATION METHOD(S):		COATS/LAYER:	FOOD SAFE? **YES NO**

BRAND:	COLOR/TRANSPARENCY/CHARACTERISTICS		
APPLICATION METHOD(S):		COATS/LAYER:	FOOD SAFE? **YES NO**

BRAND:	COLOR/TRANSPARENCY/CHARACTERISTICS		
APPLICATION METHOD(S):		COATS/LAYER:	FOOD SAFE? **YES NO**

BRAND:	COLOR/TRANSPARENCY/CHARACTERISTICS		
APPLICATION METHOD(S):		COATS/LAYER:	FOOD SAFE? **YES NO**

GLAZE FIRING 1   DATE

KILN TYPE:	PROGRAM OR FIRING METHOD:	CONE:
PREHEAT/HOLD/COOL FIRING TIME/TEMP(S):		TOTAL TIME:

GLAZE/LUSTER FIRING   DATE

KILN TYPE:	PROGRAM OR FIRING METHOD:	CONE:
PREHEAT/HOLD/COOL FIRING TIME/TEMP(S):		TOTAL TIME:

NOTES:

____

____

____

____

____

SALES RECORD

SALE LOCATION:		ESTIMATED VALUE/LISTING PRICE:
SALE DATE:	TRANSACTION DETAILS:	FINAL PRICE:

PROJECT:

DATE:

IMAGE or SKETCH

DIMENSIONS:

WEIGHT:

CLAY

TYPE:	COLOR:	SOURCE:	
ADDITIVE(S):			RESULTS RATING:

FORMING TECHNIQUE(S):

DECORATING TECHNIQUES & TOOLS:

DRYING TIME/NOTES:

BISQUE FIRING   DATE

KILN TYPE:	PROGRAM OR FIRING METHOD:	CONE:
PREHEAT/HOLD/COOL FIRING TIME/TEMP(S):		TOTAL TIME:
STAINS/SPRAYS/COMBUSTIBLES:		

Glaze(s)

BRAND:	COLOR/TRANSPARENCY/CHARACTERISTICS		
APPLICATION METHOD(S):		COATS/LAYER:	FOOD SAFE? **YES NO**

BRAND:	COLOR/TRANSPARENCY/CHARACTERISTICS		
APPLICATION METHOD(S):		COATS/LAYER:	FOOD SAFE? **YES NO**

BRAND:	COLOR/TRANSPARENCY/CHARACTERISTICS		
APPLICATION METHOD(S):		COATS/LAYER:	FOOD SAFE? **YES NO**

BRAND:	COLOR/TRANSPARENCY/CHARACTERISTICS		
APPLICATION METHOD(S):		COATS/LAYER:	FOOD SAFE? **YES NO**

BRAND:	COLOR/TRANSPARENCY/CHARACTERISTICS		
APPLICATION METHOD(S):		COATS/LAYER:	FOOD SAFE? **YES NO**

GLAZE FIRING 1   DATE

KILN TYPE:	PROGRAM OR FIRING METHOD:	CONE:
PREHEAT/HOLD/COOL FIRING TIME/TEMP(S):		TOTAL TIME:

GLAZE/LUSTER FIRING   DATE

KILN TYPE:	PROGRAM OR FIRING METHOD:	CONE:
PREHEAT/HOLD/COOL FIRING TIME/TEMP(S):		TOTAL TIME:

NOTES:

____

____

____

____

____

SALES RECORD

SALE LOCATION:	ESTIMATED VALUE/LISTING PRICE:
SALE DATE:	TRANSACTION DETAILS:	FINAL PRICE:

PROJECT: **DATE:**

IMAGE or SKETCH

DIMENSIONS: WEIGHT:

CLAY

TYPE:	COLOR:	SOURCE:	
ADDITIVE(S):			RESULTS RATING:

FORMING TECHNIQUE(S):

DECORATING TECHNIQUES & TOOLS:

DRYING TIME/NOTES:

BISQUE FIRING   DATE

KILN TYPE:	PROGRAM OR FIRING METHOD:	CONE:
PREHEAT/HOLD/COOL FIRING TIME/TEMP(S):		TOTAL TIME:
STAINS/SPRAYS/COMBUSTIBLES:		

Glaze(s)

<table>
<tr><td colspan="2">BRAND:</td><td colspan="2">COLOR/TRANSPARENCY/CHARACTERISTICS</td></tr>
<tr><td colspan="2">APPLICATION METHOD(S):</td><td>COATS/LAYER:</td><td>FOOD SAFE?
YES   NO</td></tr>
<tr><td colspan="2">BRAND:</td><td colspan="2">COLOR/TRANSPARENCY/CHARACTERISTICS</td></tr>
<tr><td colspan="2">APPLICATION METHOD(S):</td><td>COATS/LAYER:</td><td>FOOD SAFE?
YES   NO</td></tr>
<tr><td colspan="2">BRAND:</td><td colspan="2">COLOR/TRANSPARENCY/CHARACTERISTICS</td></tr>
<tr><td colspan="2">APPLICATION METHOD(S):</td><td>COATS/LAYER:</td><td>FOOD SAFE?
YES   NO</td></tr>
<tr><td colspan="2">BRAND:</td><td colspan="2">COLOR/TRANSPARENCY/CHARACTERISTICS</td></tr>
<tr><td colspan="2">APPLICATION METHOD(S):</td><td>COATS/LAYER:</td><td>FOOD SAFE?
YES   NO</td></tr>
<tr><td colspan="2">BRAND:</td><td colspan="2">COLOR/TRANSPARENCY/CHARACTERISTICS</td></tr>
<tr><td colspan="2">APPLICATION METHOD(S):</td><td>COATS/LAYER:</td><td>FOOD SAFE?
YES   NO</td></tr>
</table>

GLAZE FIRING 1   DATE

<table>
<tr><td>KILN TYPE:</td><td>PROGRAM OR FIRING METHOD:</td><td>CONE:</td></tr>
<tr><td colspan="2">PREHEAT/HOLD/COOL FIRING TIME/TEMP(S):</td><td>TOTAL TIME:</td></tr>
</table>

GLAZE/LUSTER FIRING   DATE

<table>
<tr><td>KILN TYPE:</td><td>PROGRAM OR FIRING METHOD:</td><td>CONE:</td></tr>
<tr><td colspan="2">PREHEAT/HOLD/COOL FIRING TIME/TEMP(S):</td><td>TOTAL TIME:</td></tr>
</table>

NOTES:

____

____

____

____

____

SALES RECORD

<table>
<tr><td colspan="2">SALE LOCATION:</td><td>ESTIMATED VALUE/LISTING PRICE:</td></tr>
<tr><td>SALE DATE:</td><td>TRANSACTION DETAILS:</td><td>FINAL PRICE:</td></tr>
</table>

PROJECT: ______________________   **DATE:** ______________________

IMAGE or SKETCH

DIMENSIONS: ______________________   WEIGHT: ______________________

CLAY

TYPE:	COLOR:	SOURCE:
ADDITIVE(S):		RESULTS RATING: ○ ○ ○ ○ ○

FORMING TECHNIQUE(S): ______________________
____
____

DECORATING TECHNIQUES & TOOLS: ______________________
____
____

DRYING TIME/NOTES: ______________________
____

BISQUE FIRING   DATE

KILN TYPE:	PROGRAM OR FIRING METHOD:	CONE:
PREHEAT/HOLD/COOL FIRING TIME/TEMP(S):		TOTAL TIME:
STAINS/SPRAYS/COMBUSTIBLES:		

Glaze(s)

BRAND:	COLOR/TRANSPARENCY/CHARACTERISTICS		
APPLICATION METHOD(S):		COATS/LAYER:	FOOD SAFE? YES NO

BRAND:	COLOR/TRANSPARENCY/CHARACTERISTICS		
APPLICATION METHOD(S):		COATS/LAYER:	FOOD SAFE? YES NO

BRAND:	COLOR/TRANSPARENCY/CHARACTERISTICS		
APPLICATION METHOD(S):		COATS/LAYER:	FOOD SAFE? YES NO

BRAND:	COLOR/TRANSPARENCY/CHARACTERISTICS		
APPLICATION METHOD(S):		COATS/LAYER:	FOOD SAFE? YES NO

BRAND:	COLOR/TRANSPARENCY/CHARACTERISTICS		
APPLICATION METHOD(S):		COATS/LAYER:	FOOD SAFE? YES NO

GLAZE FIRING 1   DATE

KILN TYPE:	PROGRAM OR FIRING METHOD:	CONE:
PREHEAT/HOLD/COOL FIRING TIME/TEMP(S):		TOTAL TIME:

GLAZE/LUSTER FIRING   DATE

KILN TYPE:	PROGRAM OR FIRING METHOD:	CONE:
PREHEAT/HOLD/COOL FIRING TIME/TEMP(S):		TOTAL TIME:

NOTES:

____

____

____

____

____

SALES RECORD

SALE LOCATION:		ESTIMATED VALUE/LISTING PRICE:
SALE DATE:	TRANSACTION DETAILS:	FINAL PRICE:

PROJECT: **DATE:**

IMAGE or SKETCH

DIMENSIONS: WEIGHT:

CLAY

TYPE:	COLOR:	SOURCE:
ADDITIVE(S):		RESULTS RATING:

FORMING TECHNIQUE(S):

DECORATING TECHNIQUES & TOOLS:

DRYING TIME/NOTES:

BISQUE FIRING   DATE

KILN TYPE:	PROGRAM OR FIRING METHOD:	CONE:
PREHEAT/HOLD/COOL FIRING TIME/TEMP(S):		TOTAL TIME:
STAINS/SPRAYS/COMBUSTIBLES:		

Glaze(s)

BRAND:	COLOR/TRANSPARENCY/CHARACTERISTICS		
APPLICATION METHOD(S):		COATS/LAYER:	FOOD SAFE? **YES NO**

BRAND:	COLOR/TRANSPARENCY/CHARACTERISTICS		
APPLICATION METHOD(S):		COATS/LAYER:	FOOD SAFE? **YES NO**

BRAND:	COLOR/TRANSPARENCY/CHARACTERISTICS		
APPLICATION METHOD(S):		COATS/LAYER:	FOOD SAFE? **YES NO**

BRAND:	COLOR/TRANSPARENCY/CHARACTERISTICS		
APPLICATION METHOD(S):		COATS/LAYER:	FOOD SAFE? **YES NO**

BRAND:	COLOR/TRANSPARENCY/CHARACTERISTICS		
APPLICATION METHOD(S):		COATS/LAYER:	FOOD SAFE? **YES NO**

GLAZE FIRING 1   DATE

KILN TYPE:	PROGRAM OR FIRING METHOD:	CONE:
PREHEAT/HOLD/COOL FIRING TIME/TEMP(S):		TOTAL TIME:

GLAZE/LUSTER FIRING   DATE

KILN TYPE:	PROGRAM OR FIRING METHOD:	CONE:
PREHEAT/HOLD/COOL FIRING TIME/TEMP(S):		TOTAL TIME:

NOTES:

____

____

____

____

____

SALES RECORD

SALE LOCATION:		ESTIMATED VALUE/LISTING PRICE:
SALE DATE:	TRANSACTION DETAILS:	FINAL PRICE:

PROJECT: **DATE:**

IMAGE or SKETCH

DIMENSIONS: WEIGHT:

CLAY

TYPE:	COLOR:	SOURCE:
ADDITIVE(S):		RESULTS RATING:

FORMING TECHNIQUE(S):

DECORATING TECHNIQUES & TOOLS:

DRYING TIME/NOTES:

BISQUE FIRING   DATE

KILN TYPE:	PROGRAM OR FIRING METHOD:	CONE:
PREHEAT/HOLD/COOL FIRING TIME/TEMP(S):		TOTAL TIME:
STAINS/SPRAYS/COMBUSTIBLES:		

Glaze(s)

BRAND:	COLOR/TRANSPARENCY/CHARACTERISTICS		
APPLICATION METHOD(S):		COATS/LAYER:	FOOD SAFE? **YES NO**

BRAND:	COLOR/TRANSPARENCY/CHARACTERISTICS		
APPLICATION METHOD(S):		COATS/LAYER:	FOOD SAFE? **YES NO**

BRAND:	COLOR/TRANSPARENCY/CHARACTERISTICS		
APPLICATION METHOD(S):		COATS/LAYER:	FOOD SAFE? **YES NO**

BRAND:	COLOR/TRANSPARENCY/CHARACTERISTICS		
APPLICATION METHOD(S):		COATS/LAYER:	FOOD SAFE? **YES NO**

BRAND:	COLOR/TRANSPARENCY/CHARACTERISTICS		
APPLICATION METHOD(S):		COATS/LAYER:	FOOD SAFE? **YES NO**

GLAZE FIRING 1   DATE

KILN TYPE:	PROGRAM OR FIRING METHOD:	CONE:
PREHEAT/HOLD/COOL FIRING TIME/TEMP(S):		TOTAL TIME:

GLAZE/LUSTER FIRING   DATE

KILN TYPE:	PROGRAM OR FIRING METHOD:	CONE:
PREHEAT/HOLD/COOL FIRING TIME/TEMP(S):		TOTAL TIME:

NOTES:

____

____

____

____

____

SALES RECORD

SALE LOCATION:		ESTIMATED VALUE/LISTING PRICE:
SALE DATE:	TRANSACTION DETAILS:	FINAL PRICE:

PROJECT: **DATE:**

IMAGE or SKETCH

DIMENSIONS: WEIGHT:

CLAY

TYPE:	COLOR:	SOURCE:
ADDITIVE(S):		RESULTS RATING:

FORMING TECHNIQUE(S):

DECORATING TECHNIQUES & TOOLS:

DRYING TIME/NOTES:

BISQUE FIRING   DATE

KILN TYPE:	PROGRAM OR FIRING METHOD:	CONE:
PREHEAT/HOLD/COOL FIRING TIME/TEMP(S):		TOTAL TIME:
STAINS/SPRAYS/COMBUSTIBLES:		

Glaze(s)

BRAND:	COLOR/TRANSPARENCY/CHARACTERISTICS		
APPLICATION METHOD(S):		COATS/LAYER:	FOOD SAFE? **YES NO**

BRAND:	COLOR/TRANSPARENCY/CHARACTERISTICS		
APPLICATION METHOD(S):		COATS/LAYER:	FOOD SAFE? **YES NO**

BRAND:	COLOR/TRANSPARENCY/CHARACTERISTICS		
APPLICATION METHOD(S):		COATS/LAYER:	FOOD SAFE? **YES NO**

BRAND:	COLOR/TRANSPARENCY/CHARACTERISTICS		
APPLICATION METHOD(S):		COATS/LAYER:	FOOD SAFE? **YES NO**

BRAND:	COLOR/TRANSPARENCY/CHARACTERISTICS		
APPLICATION METHOD(S):		COATS/LAYER:	FOOD SAFE? **YES NO**

GLAZE FIRING 1   DATE

KILN TYPE:	PROGRAM OR FIRING METHOD:	CONE:
PREHEAT/HOLD/COOL FIRING TIME/TEMP(S):		TOTAL TIME:

GLAZE/LUSTER FIRING   DATE

KILN TYPE:	PROGRAM OR FIRING METHOD:	CONE:
PREHEAT/HOLD/COOL FIRING TIME/TEMP(S):		TOTAL TIME:

NOTES:

____

____

____

____

____

SALES RECORD

SALE LOCATION:	ESTIMATED VALUE/LISTING PRICE:
SALE DATE:	TRANSACTION DETAILS:	FINAL PRICE:

PROJECT: **DATE:**

IMAGE or SKETCH

DIMENSIONS: WEIGHT:

CLAY

TYPE:	COLOR:	SOURCE:
ADDITIVE(S):		RESULTS RATING:

FORMING TECHNIQUE(S):

DECORATING TECHNIQUES & TOOLS:

DRYING TIME/NOTES:

BISQUE FIRING   DATE

KILN TYPE:	PROGRAM OR FIRING METHOD:	CONE:
PREHEAT/HOLD/COOL FIRING TIME/TEMP(S):		TOTAL TIME:
STAINS/SPRAYS/COMBUSTIBLES:		

Glaze(s)

BRAND:	COLOR/TRANSPARENCY/CHARACTERISTICS		
APPLICATION METHOD(S):		COATS/LAYER:	FOOD SAFE? **YES NO**

BRAND:	COLOR/TRANSPARENCY/CHARACTERISTICS		
APPLICATION METHOD(S):		COATS/LAYER:	FOOD SAFE? **YES NO**

BRAND:	COLOR/TRANSPARENCY/CHARACTERISTICS		
APPLICATION METHOD(S):		COATS/LAYER:	FOOD SAFE? **YES NO**

BRAND:	COLOR/TRANSPARENCY/CHARACTERISTICS		
APPLICATION METHOD(S):		COATS/LAYER:	FOOD SAFE? **YES NO**

BRAND:	COLOR/TRANSPARENCY/CHARACTERISTICS		
APPLICATION METHOD(S):		COATS/LAYER:	FOOD SAFE? **YES NO**

GLAZE FIRING 1   DATE

KILN TYPE:	PROGRAM OR FIRING METHOD:	CONE:
PREHEAT/HOLD/COOL FIRING TIME/TEMP(S):		TOTAL TIME:

GLAZE/LUSTER FIRING   DATE

KILN TYPE:	PROGRAM OR FIRING METHOD:	CONE:
PREHEAT/HOLD/COOL FIRING TIME/TEMP(S):		TOTAL TIME:

NOTES:

____

____

____

____

____

SALES RECORD

SALE LOCATION:	ESTIMATED VALUE/LISTING PRICE:	
SALE DATE:	TRANSACTION DETAILS:	FINAL PRICE:

PROJECT: **DATE:**

IMAGE or SKETCH

DIMENSIONS: **WEIGHT:**

CLAY

TYPE:	COLOR:	SOURCE:	
ADDITIVE(S):			RESULTS RATING:

FORMING TECHNIQUE(S):

DECORATING TECHNIQUES & TOOLS:

DRYING TIME/NOTES:

BISQUE FIRING   DATE

KILN TYPE:	PROGRAM OR FIRING METHOD:	CONE:
PREHEAT/HOLD/COOL FIRING TIME/TEMP(S):		TOTAL TIME:
STAINS/SPRAYS/COMBUSTIBLES:		

Glaze(s)

BRAND:	COLOR/TRANSPARENCY/CHARACTERISTICS		
APPLICATION METHOD(S):		COATS/LAYER:	FOOD SAFE? **YES NO**

BRAND:	COLOR/TRANSPARENCY/CHARACTERISTICS		
APPLICATION METHOD(S):		COATS/LAYER:	FOOD SAFE? **YES NO**

BRAND:	COLOR/TRANSPARENCY/CHARACTERISTICS		
APPLICATION METHOD(S):		COATS/LAYER:	FOOD SAFE? **YES NO**

BRAND:	COLOR/TRANSPARENCY/CHARACTERISTICS		
APPLICATION METHOD(S):		COATS/LAYER:	FOOD SAFE? **YES NO**

BRAND:	COLOR/TRANSPARENCY/CHARACTERISTICS		
APPLICATION METHOD(S):		COATS/LAYER:	FOOD SAFE? **YES NO**

GLAZE FIRING 1   DATE

KILN TYPE:	PROGRAM OR FIRING METHOD:	CONE:
PREHEAT/HOLD/COOL FIRING TIME/TEMP(S):		TOTAL TIME:

GLAZE/LUSTER FIRING   DATE

KILN TYPE:	PROGRAM OR FIRING METHOD:	CONE:
PREHEAT/HOLD/COOL FIRING TIME/TEMP(S):		TOTAL TIME:

NOTES:

____

____

____

____

____

SALES RECORD

SALE LOCATION:		ESTIMATED VALUE/LISTING PRICE:
SALE DATE:	TRANSACTION DETAILS:	FINAL PRICE:

PROJECT: ___________________________   **DATE:** ___________________________

IMAGE or SKETCH

DIMENSIONS: ___________________________   WEIGHT: ___________________________

CLAY

TYPE:	COLOR:	SOURCE:
ADDITIVE(S):		RESULTS RATING:

FORMING TECHNIQUE(S):
____
____

DECORATING TECHNIQUES & TOOLS:
____
____

DRYING TIME/NOTES:
____

BISQUE FIRING   DATE

KILN TYPE:	PROGRAM OR FIRING METHOD:	CONE:
PREHEAT/HOLD/COOL FIRING TIME/TEMP(S):		TOTAL TIME:
STAINS/SPRAYS/COMBUSTIBLES:		

Glaze(s)

BRAND:	COLOR/TRANSPARENCY/CHARACTERISTICS		
APPLICATION METHOD(S):		COATS/LAYER:	FOOD SAFE? **YES NO**

BRAND:	COLOR/TRANSPARENCY/CHARACTERISTICS		
APPLICATION METHOD(S):		COATS/LAYER:	FOOD SAFE? **YES NO**

BRAND:	COLOR/TRANSPARENCY/CHARACTERISTICS		
APPLICATION METHOD(S):		COATS/LAYER:	FOOD SAFE? **YES NO**

BRAND:	COLOR/TRANSPARENCY/CHARACTERISTICS		
APPLICATION METHOD(S):		COATS/LAYER:	FOOD SAFE? **YES NO**

BRAND:	COLOR/TRANSPARENCY/CHARACTERISTICS		
APPLICATION METHOD(S):		COATS/LAYER:	FOOD SAFE? **YES NO**

GLAZE FIRING 1   DATE

KILN TYPE:	PROGRAM OR FIRING METHOD:	CONE:
PREHEAT/HOLD/COOL FIRING TIME/TEMP(S):		TOTAL TIME:

GLAZE/LUSTER FIRING   DATE

KILN TYPE:	PROGRAM OR FIRING METHOD:	CONE:
PREHEAT/HOLD/COOL FIRING TIME/TEMP(S):		TOTAL TIME:

NOTES:

____

____

____

____

____

SALES RECORD

SALE LOCATION:	ESTIMATED VALUE/LISTING PRICE:
SALE DATE:	TRANSACTION DETAILS:	FINAL PRICE:

PROJECT: **DATE:**

IMAGE or SKETCH

DIMENSIONS: **WEIGHT:**

CLAY

TYPE:	COLOR:	SOURCE:
ADDITIVE(S):		RESULTS RATING:

FORMING TECHNIQUE(S):

DECORATING TECHNIQUES & TOOLS:

DRYING TIME/NOTES:

BISQUE FIRING   DATE

KILN TYPE:	PROGRAM OR FIRING METHOD:	CONE:
PREHEAT/HOLD/COOL FIRING TIME/TEMP(S):		TOTAL TIME:
STAINS/SPRAYS/COMBUSTIBLES:		

Glaze(s)

BRAND:	COLOR/TRANSPARENCY/CHARACTERISTICS		
APPLICATION METHOD(S):		COATS/LAYER:	FOOD SAFE? **YES NO**

BRAND:	COLOR/TRANSPARENCY/CHARACTERISTICS		
APPLICATION METHOD(S):		COATS/LAYER:	FOOD SAFE? **YES NO**

BRAND:	COLOR/TRANSPARENCY/CHARACTERISTICS		
APPLICATION METHOD(S):		COATS/LAYER:	FOOD SAFE? **YES NO**

BRAND:	COLOR/TRANSPARENCY/CHARACTERISTICS		
APPLICATION METHOD(S):		COATS/LAYER:	FOOD SAFE? **YES NO**

BRAND:	COLOR/TRANSPARENCY/CHARACTERISTICS		
APPLICATION METHOD(S):		COATS/LAYER:	FOOD SAFE? **YES NO**

GLAZE FIRING 1   DATE

KILN TYPE:	PROGRAM OR FIRING METHOD:	CONE:
PREHEAT/HOLD/COOL FIRING TIME/TEMP(S):		TOTAL TIME:

GLAZE/LUSTER FIRING   DATE

KILN TYPE:	PROGRAM OR FIRING METHOD:	CONE:
PREHEAT/HOLD/COOL FIRING TIME/TEMP(S):		TOTAL TIME:

NOTES:

____

____

____

____

____

SALES RECORD

SALE LOCATION:	ESTIMATED VALUE/LISTING PRICE:	
SALE DATE:	TRANSACTION DETAILS:	FINAL PRICE:

PROJECT: | **DATE:**

IMAGE or SKETCH

DIMENSIONS: | WEIGHT:

CLAY

TYPE:		COLOR:	SOURCE:	
ADDITIVE(S):				RESULTS RATING:

FORMING TECHNIQUE(S):

DECORATING TECHNIQUES & TOOLS:

DRYING TIME/NOTES:

BISQUE FIRING   DATE

KILN TYPE:	PROGRAM OR FIRING METHOD:	CONE:
PREHEAT/HOLD/COOL FIRING TIME/TEMP(S):		TOTAL TIME:
STAINS/SPRAYS/COMBUSTIBLES:		

Glaze(s)

BRAND:	COLOR/TRANSPARENCY/CHARACTERISTICS		
APPLICATION METHOD(S):		COATS/LAYER:	FOOD SAFE? **YES NO**

BRAND:	COLOR/TRANSPARENCY/CHARACTERISTICS		
APPLICATION METHOD(S):		COATS/LAYER:	FOOD SAFE? **YES NO**

BRAND:	COLOR/TRANSPARENCY/CHARACTERISTICS		
APPLICATION METHOD(S):		COATS/LAYER:	FOOD SAFE? **YES NO**

BRAND:	COLOR/TRANSPARENCY/CHARACTERISTICS		
APPLICATION METHOD(S):		COATS/LAYER:	FOOD SAFE? **YES NO**

BRAND:	COLOR/TRANSPARENCY/CHARACTERISTICS		
APPLICATION METHOD(S):		COATS/LAYER:	FOOD SAFE? **YES NO**

GLAZE FIRING 1   DATE

KILN TYPE:	PROGRAM OR FIRING METHOD:	CONE:
PREHEAT/HOLD/COOL FIRING TIME/TEMP(S):		TOTAL TIME:

GLAZE/LUSTER FIRING   DATE

KILN TYPE:	PROGRAM OR FIRING METHOD:	CONE:
PREHEAT/HOLD/COOL FIRING TIME/TEMP(S):		TOTAL TIME:

NOTES:

____

____

____

____

____

SALES RECORD

SALE LOCATION:	ESTIMATED VALUE/LISTING PRICE:
SALE DATE: TRANSACTION DETAILS:	FINAL PRICE:

PROJECT: **DATE:**

DIMENSIONS: WEIGHT:

CLAY

TYPE:		COLOR:	SOURCE:	
ADDITIVE(S):				RESULTS RATING:

FORMING TECHNIQUE(S):

DECORATING TECHNIQUES & TOOLS:

DRYING TIME/NOTES:

BISQUE FIRING   DATE

KILN TYPE:	PROGRAM OR FIRING METHOD:		CONE:
PREHEAT/HOLD/COOL FIRING TIME/TEMP(S):			TOTAL TIME:
STAINS/SPRAYS/COMBUSTIBLES:			

Glaze(s)

BRAND:	COLOR/TRANSPARENCY/CHARACTERISTICS		
APPLICATION METHOD(S):		COATS/LAYER:	FOOD SAFE? **YES NO**
BRAND:	COLOR/TRANSPARENCY/CHARACTERISTICS		
APPLICATION METHOD(S):		COATS/LAYER:	FOOD SAFE? **YES NO**
BRAND:	COLOR/TRANSPARENCY/CHARACTERISTICS		
APPLICATION METHOD(S):		COATS/LAYER:	FOOD SAFE? **YES NO**
BRAND:	COLOR/TRANSPARENCY/CHARACTERISTICS		
APPLICATION METHOD(S):		COATS/LAYER:	FOOD SAFE? **YES NO**
BRAND:	COLOR/TRANSPARENCY/CHARACTERISTICS		
APPLICATION METHOD(S):		COATS/LAYER:	FOOD SAFE? **YES NO**

GLAZE FIRING 1   DATE

KILN TYPE:	PROGRAM OR FIRING METHOD:	CONE:
PREHEAT/HOLD/COOL FIRING TIME/TEMP(S):		TOTAL TIME:

GLAZE/LUSTER FIRING   DATE

KILN TYPE:	PROGRAM OR FIRING METHOD:	CONE:
PREHEAT/HOLD/COOL FIRING TIME/TEMP(S):		TOTAL TIME:

NOTES:

____

____

____

____

____

SALES RECORD

SALE LOCATION:		ESTIMATED VALUE/LISTING PRICE:
SALE DATE:	TRANSACTION DETAILS:	FINAL PRICE:

PROJECT:

DATE:

IMAGE or SKETCH

DIMENSIONS:

WEIGHT:

CLAY

TYPE:	COLOR:	SOURCE:

ADDITIVE(S):	RESULTS RATING:

FORMING TECHNIQUE(S):

DECORATING TECHNIQUES & TOOLS:

DRYING TIME/NOTES:

BISQUE FIRING   DATE

KILN TYPE:	PROGRAM OR FIRING METHOD:	CONE:

PREHEAT/HOLD/COOL FIRING TIME/TEMP(S):	TOTAL TIME:

STAINS/SPRAYS/COMBUSTIBLES:

Glaze(s)

<table>
<tr><td>BRAND:</td><td colspan="2">COLOR/TRANSPARENCY/CHARACTERISTICS</td></tr>
<tr><td>APPLICATION METHOD(S):</td><td>COATS/LAYER:</td><td>FOOD SAFE?
YES   NO</td></tr>
</table>

<table>
<tr><td>BRAND:</td><td colspan="2">COLOR/TRANSPARENCY/CHARACTERISTICS</td></tr>
<tr><td>APPLICATION METHOD(S):</td><td>COATS/LAYER:</td><td>FOOD SAFE?
YES   NO</td></tr>
</table>

<table>
<tr><td>BRAND:</td><td colspan="2">COLOR/TRANSPARENCY/CHARACTERISTICS</td></tr>
<tr><td>APPLICATION METHOD(S):</td><td>COATS/LAYER:</td><td>FOOD SAFE?
YES   NO</td></tr>
</table>

<table>
<tr><td>BRAND:</td><td colspan="2">COLOR/TRANSPARENCY/CHARACTERISTICS</td></tr>
<tr><td>APPLICATION METHOD(S):</td><td>COATS/LAYER:</td><td>FOOD SAFE?
YES   NO</td></tr>
</table>

<table>
<tr><td>BRAND:</td><td colspan="2">COLOR/TRANSPARENCY/CHARACTERISTICS</td></tr>
<tr><td>APPLICATION METHOD(S):</td><td>COATS/LAYER:</td><td>FOOD SAFE?
YES   NO</td></tr>
</table>

GLAZE FIRING 1   DATE

<table>
<tr><td>KILN TYPE:</td><td>PROGRAM OR FIRING METHOD:</td><td>CONE:</td></tr>
<tr><td>PREHEAT/HOLD/COOL FIRING TIME/TEMP(S):</td><td></td><td>TOTAL TIME:</td></tr>
</table>

GLAZE/LUSTER FIRING   DATE

<table>
<tr><td>KILN TYPE:</td><td>PROGRAM OR FIRING METHOD:</td><td>CONE:</td></tr>
<tr><td>PREHEAT/HOLD/COOL FIRING TIME/TEMP(S):</td><td></td><td>TOTAL TIME:</td></tr>
</table>

NOTES:

____

____

____

____

____

SALES RECORD

<table>
<tr><td>SALE LOCATION:</td><td>ESTIMATED VALUE/LISTING PRICE:</td></tr>
<tr><td>SALE DATE:</td><td>TRANSACTION DETAILS:</td><td>FINAL PRICE:</td></tr>
</table>

PROJECT: **DATE:**

IMAGE or SKETCH

DIMENSIONS: WEIGHT:

CLAY

TYPE:	COLOR:	SOURCE:
ADDITIVE(S):		RESULTS RATING:

FORMING TECHNIQUE(S):

DECORATING TECHNIQUES & TOOLS:

DRYING TIME/NOTES:

BISQUE FIRING   DATE

KILN TYPE:	PROGRAM OR FIRING METHOD:	CONE:
PREHEAT/HOLD/COOL FIRING TIME/TEMP(S):		TOTAL TIME:
STAINS/SPRAYS/COMBUSTIBLES:		

Glaze(s)

BRAND:	COLOR/TRANSPARENCY/CHARACTERISTICS		
APPLICATION METHOD(S):		COATS/LAYER:	FOOD SAFE? **YES NO**

BRAND:	COLOR/TRANSPARENCY/CHARACTERISTICS		
APPLICATION METHOD(S):		COATS/LAYER:	FOOD SAFE? **YES NO**

BRAND:	COLOR/TRANSPARENCY/CHARACTERISTICS		
APPLICATION METHOD(S):		COATS/LAYER:	FOOD SAFE? **YES NO**

BRAND:	COLOR/TRANSPARENCY/CHARACTERISTICS		
APPLICATION METHOD(S):		COATS/LAYER:	FOOD SAFE? **YES NO**

BRAND:	COLOR/TRANSPARENCY/CHARACTERISTICS		
APPLICATION METHOD(S):		COATS/LAYER:	FOOD SAFE? **YES NO**

GLAZE FIRING 1   DATE

KILN TYPE:	PROGRAM OR FIRING METHOD:	CONE:
PREHEAT/HOLD/COOL FIRING TIME/TEMP(S):		TOTAL TIME:

GLAZE/LUSTER FIRING   DATE

KILN TYPE:	PROGRAM OR FIRING METHOD:	CONE:
PREHEAT/HOLD/COOL FIRING TIME/TEMP(S):		TOTAL TIME:

NOTES:

____

____

____

____

SALES RECORD

SALE LOCATION:	ESTIMATED VALUE/LISTING PRICE:
SALE DATE:	TRANSACTION DETAILS:	FINAL PRICE:

PROJECT: **DATE:**

IMAGE or SKETCH

DIMENSIONS: **WEIGHT:**

CLAY

TYPE:	COLOR:	SOURCE:
ADDITIVE(S):		RESULTS RATING:

FORMING TECHNIQUE(S):

DECORATING TECHNIQUES & TOOLS:

DRYING TIME/NOTES:

BISQUE FIRING   DATE

KILN TYPE:	PROGRAM OR FIRING METHOD:	CONE:
PREHEAT/HOLD/COOL FIRING TIME/TEMP(S):		TOTAL TIME:
STAINS/SPRAYS/COMBUSTIBLES:		

Glaze(s)

BRAND:	COLOR/TRANSPARENCY/CHARACTERISTICS		
APPLICATION METHOD(S):		COATS/LAYER:	FOOD SAFE? **YES NO**

BRAND:	COLOR/TRANSPARENCY/CHARACTERISTICS		
APPLICATION METHOD(S):		COATS/LAYER:	FOOD SAFE? **YES NO**

BRAND:	COLOR/TRANSPARENCY/CHARACTERISTICS		
APPLICATION METHOD(S):		COATS/LAYER:	FOOD SAFE? **YES NO**

BRAND:	COLOR/TRANSPARENCY/CHARACTERISTICS		
APPLICATION METHOD(S):		COATS/LAYER:	FOOD SAFE? **YES NO**

BRAND:	COLOR/TRANSPARENCY/CHARACTERISTICS		
APPLICATION METHOD(S):		COATS/LAYER:	FOOD SAFE? **YES NO**

GLAZE FIRING 1   DATE

KILN TYPE:	PROGRAM OR FIRING METHOD:	CONE:
PREHEAT/HOLD/COOL FIRING TIME/TEMP(S):		TOTAL TIME:

GLAZE/LUSTER FIRING   DATE

KILN TYPE:	PROGRAM OR FIRING METHOD:	CONE:
PREHEAT/HOLD/COOL FIRING TIME/TEMP(S):		TOTAL TIME:

NOTES:

____

____

____

____

____

SALES RECORD

SALE LOCATION:	ESTIMATED VALUE/LISTING PRICE:

SALE DATE:	TRANSACTION DETAILS:	FINAL PRICE:

PROJECT: **DATE:**

IMAGE or SKETCH

DIMENSIONS: WEIGHT:

CLAY

TYPE:	COLOR:	SOURCE:
ADDITIVE(S):		RESULTS RATING:

FORMING TECHNIQUE(S):

DECORATING TECHNIQUES & TOOLS:

DRYING TIME/NOTES:

BISQUE FIRING   DATE

KILN TYPE:	PROGRAM OR FIRING METHOD:	CONE:
PREHEAT/HOLD/COOL FIRING TIME/TEMP(S):		TOTAL TIME:
STAINS/SPRAYS/COMBUSTIBLES:		

Glaze(s)

BRAND:	COLOR/TRANSPARENCY/CHARACTERISTICS		
APPLICATION METHOD(S):		COATS/LAYER:	FOOD SAFE? **YES NO**

BRAND:	COLOR/TRANSPARENCY/CHARACTERISTICS		
APPLICATION METHOD(S):		COATS/LAYER:	FOOD SAFE? **YES NO**

BRAND:	COLOR/TRANSPARENCY/CHARACTERISTICS		
APPLICATION METHOD(S):		COATS/LAYER:	FOOD SAFE? **YES NO**

BRAND:	COLOR/TRANSPARENCY/CHARACTERISTICS		
APPLICATION METHOD(S):		COATS/LAYER:	FOOD SAFE? **YES NO**

BRAND:	COLOR/TRANSPARENCY/CHARACTERISTICS		
APPLICATION METHOD(S):		COATS/LAYER:	FOOD SAFE? **YES NO**

GLAZE FIRING 1   DATE

KILN TYPE:	PROGRAM OR FIRING METHOD:	CONE:
PREHEAT/HOLD/COOL FIRING TIME/TEMP(S):		TOTAL TIME:

GLAZE/LUSTER FIRING   DATE

KILN TYPE:	PROGRAM OR FIRING METHOD:	CONE:
PREHEAT/HOLD/COOL FIRING TIME/TEMP(S):		TOTAL TIME:

NOTES:

____

____

____

____

____

SALES RECORD

SALE LOCATION:	ESTIMATED VALUE/LISTING PRICE:
SALE DATE:	TRANSACTION DETAILS:	FINAL PRICE:

PROJECT: **DATE:**

IMAGE or SKETCH

DIMENSIONS: WEIGHT:

CLAY

TYPE:		COLOR:	SOURCE:	
ADDITIVE(S):				RESULTS RATING:

FORMING TECHNIQUE(S):

____

____

DECORATING TECHNIQUES & TOOLS:

____

____

DRYING TIME/NOTES:

____

BISQUE FIRING   DATE

KILN TYPE:	PROGRAM OR FIRING METHOD:	CONE:
PREHEAT/HOLD/COOL FIRING TIME/TEMP(S):		TOTAL TIME:
STAINS/SPRAYS/COMBUSTIBLES:		

Glaze(s)

BRAND:	COLOR/TRANSPARENCY/CHARACTERISTICS		
APPLICATION METHOD(S):		COATS/LAYER:	FOOD SAFE? **YES NO**

BRAND:	COLOR/TRANSPARENCY/CHARACTERISTICS		
APPLICATION METHOD(S):		COATS/LAYER:	FOOD SAFE? **YES NO**

BRAND:	COLOR/TRANSPARENCY/CHARACTERISTICS		
APPLICATION METHOD(S):		COATS/LAYER:	FOOD SAFE? **YES NO**

BRAND:	COLOR/TRANSPARENCY/CHARACTERISTICS		
APPLICATION METHOD(S):		COATS/LAYER:	FOOD SAFE? **YES NO**

BRAND:	COLOR/TRANSPARENCY/CHARACTERISTICS		
APPLICATION METHOD(S):		COATS/LAYER:	FOOD SAFE? **YES NO**

GLAZE FIRING 1   DATE

KILN TYPE:	PROGRAM OR FIRING METHOD:	CONE:
PREHEAT/HOLD/COOL FIRING TIME/TEMP(S):		TOTAL TIME:

GLAZE/LUSTER FIRING   DATE

KILN TYPE:	PROGRAM OR FIRING METHOD:	CONE:
PREHEAT/HOLD/COOL FIRING TIME/TEMP(S):		TOTAL TIME:

NOTES:

____

____

____

____

SALES RECORD

SALE LOCATION:	ESTIMATED VALUE/LISTING PRICE:
SALE DATE: TRANSACTION DETAILS:	FINAL PRICE:

PROJECT: **DATE:**

DIMENSIONS: WEIGHT:

CLAY

TYPE:	COLOR:	SOURCE:
ADDITIVE(S):		RESULTS RATING:

FORMING TECHNIQUE(S):

____

____

DECORATING TECHNIQUES & TOOLS:

____

____

DRYING TIME/NOTES:

____

BISQUE FIRING   DATE

KILN TYPE:	PROGRAM OR FIRING METHOD:	CONE:
PREHEAT/HOLD/COOL FIRING TIME/TEMP(S):		TOTAL TIME:
STAINS/SPRAYS/COMBUSTIBLES:		

Glaze(s)

BRAND:	COLOR/TRANSPARENCY/CHARACTERISTICS		
APPLICATION METHOD(S):		COATS/LAYER:	FOOD SAFE? **YES NO**

BRAND:	COLOR/TRANSPARENCY/CHARACTERISTICS		
APPLICATION METHOD(S):		COATS/LAYER:	FOOD SAFE? **YES NO**

BRAND:	COLOR/TRANSPARENCY/CHARACTERISTICS		
APPLICATION METHOD(S):		COATS/LAYER:	FOOD SAFE? **YES NO**

BRAND:	COLOR/TRANSPARENCY/CHARACTERISTICS		
APPLICATION METHOD(S):		COATS/LAYER:	FOOD SAFE? **YES NO**

BRAND:	COLOR/TRANSPARENCY/CHARACTERISTICS		
APPLICATION METHOD(S):		COATS/LAYER:	FOOD SAFE? **YES NO**

GLAZE FIRING 1   DATE

KILN TYPE:	PROGRAM OR FIRING METHOD:	CONE:
PREHEAT/HOLD/COOL FIRING TIME/TEMP(S):		TOTAL TIME:

GLAZE/LUSTER FIRING   DATE

KILN TYPE:	PROGRAM OR FIRING METHOD:	CONE:
PREHEAT/HOLD/COOL FIRING TIME/TEMP(S):		TOTAL TIME:

NOTES:

____

____

____

____

____

SALES RECORD

SALE LOCATION:		ESTIMATED VALUE/LISTING PRICE:
SALE DATE:	TRANSACTION DETAILS:	FINAL PRICE:

PROJECT: **DATE:**

IMAGE or SKETCH

DIMENSIONS: WEIGHT:

CLAY

TYPE:	COLOR:	SOURCE:

ADDITIVE(S):	RESULTS RATING:

FORMING TECHNIQUE(S):

DECORATING TECHNIQUES & TOOLS:

DRYING TIME/NOTES:

BISQUE FIRING   DATE

KILN TYPE:	PROGRAM OR FIRING METHOD:	CONE:

PREHEAT/HOLD/COOL FIRING TIME/TEMP(S):	TOTAL TIME:

STAINS/SPRAYS/COMBUSTIBLES:

Glaze(s)

BRAND:	COLOR/TRANSPARENCY/CHARACTERISTICS		
APPLICATION METHOD(S):		COATS/LAYER:	FOOD SAFE? **YES NO**

BRAND:	COLOR/TRANSPARENCY/CHARACTERISTICS		
APPLICATION METHOD(S):		COATS/LAYER:	FOOD SAFE? **YES NO**

BRAND:	COLOR/TRANSPARENCY/CHARACTERISTICS		
APPLICATION METHOD(S):		COATS/LAYER:	FOOD SAFE? **YES NO**

BRAND:	COLOR/TRANSPARENCY/CHARACTERISTICS		
APPLICATION METHOD(S):		COATS/LAYER:	FOOD SAFE? **YES NO**

BRAND:	COLOR/TRANSPARENCY/CHARACTERISTICS		
APPLICATION METHOD(S):		COATS/LAYER:	FOOD SAFE? **YES NO**

GLAZE FIRING 1   DATE

KILN TYPE:	PROGRAM OR FIRING METHOD:	CONE:
PREHEAT/HOLD/COOL FIRING TIME/TEMP(S):		TOTAL TIME:

GLAZE/LUSTER FIRING   DATE

KILN TYPE:	PROGRAM OR FIRING METHOD:	CONE:
PREHEAT/HOLD/COOL FIRING TIME/TEMP(S):		TOTAL TIME:

NOTES:

____

____

____

____

____

SALES RECORD

SALE LOCATION:	ESTIMATED VALUE/LISTING PRICE:
SALE DATE: TRANSACTION DETAILS:	FINAL PRICE:

PROJECT: **DATE:**

IMAGE or SKETCH

DIMENSIONS: **WEIGHT:**

CLAY

TYPE:	COLOR:	SOURCE:

ADDITIVE(S):	RESULTS RATING:

FORMING TECHNIQUE(S):

DECORATING TECHNIQUES & TOOLS:

DRYING TIME/NOTES:

BISQUE FIRING   DATE

KILN TYPE:	PROGRAM OR FIRING METHOD:	CONE:
PREHEAT/HOLD/COOL FIRING TIME/TEMP(S):		TOTAL TIME:
STAINS/SPRAYS/COMBUSTIBLES:		

Glaze(s)

BRAND:	COLOR/TRANSPARENCY/CHARACTERISTICS		
APPLICATION METHOD(S):		COATS/LAYER:	FOOD SAFE? **YES NO**

BRAND:	COLOR/TRANSPARENCY/CHARACTERISTICS		
APPLICATION METHOD(S):		COATS/LAYER:	FOOD SAFE? **YES NO**

BRAND:	COLOR/TRANSPARENCY/CHARACTERISTICS		
APPLICATION METHOD(S):		COATS/LAYER:	FOOD SAFE? **YES NO**

BRAND:	COLOR/TRANSPARENCY/CHARACTERISTICS		
APPLICATION METHOD(S):		COATS/LAYER:	FOOD SAFE? **YES NO**

BRAND:	COLOR/TRANSPARENCY/CHARACTERISTICS		
APPLICATION METHOD(S):		COATS/LAYER:	FOOD SAFE? **YES NO**

GLAZE FIRING 1   DATE

KILN TYPE:	PROGRAM OR FIRING METHOD:	CONE:
PREHEAT/HOLD/COOL FIRING TIME/TEMP(S):		TOTAL TIME:

GLAZE/LUSTER FIRING   DATE

KILN TYPE:	PROGRAM OR FIRING METHOD:	CONE:
PREHEAT/HOLD/COOL FIRING TIME/TEMP(S):		TOTAL TIME:

NOTES:

____

____

____

____

____

SALES RECORD

SALE LOCATION:	ESTIMATED VALUE/LISTING PRICE:
SALE DATE:	TRANSACTION DETAILS:	FINAL PRICE:

PROJECT: **DATE:**

IMAGE or SKETCH

DIMENSIONS: WEIGHT:

CLAY

TYPE:	COLOR:	SOURCE:
ADDITIVE(S):		RESULTS RATING:

FORMING TECHNIQUE(S):

DECORATING TECHNIQUES & TOOLS:

DRYING TIME/NOTES:

BISQUE FIRING   DATE

KILN TYPE:	PROGRAM OR FIRING METHOD:	CONE:
PREHEAT/HOLD/COOL FIRING TIME/TEMP(S):		TOTAL TIME:
STAINS/SPRAYS/COMBUSTIBLES:		

Glaze(s)

BRAND:	COLOR/TRANSPARENCY/CHARACTERISTICS		
APPLICATION METHOD(S):		COATS/LAYER:	FOOD SAFE? **YES NO**

BRAND:	COLOR/TRANSPARENCY/CHARACTERISTICS		
APPLICATION METHOD(S):		COATS/LAYER:	FOOD SAFE? **YES NO**

BRAND:	COLOR/TRANSPARENCY/CHARACTERISTICS		
APPLICATION METHOD(S):		COATS/LAYER:	FOOD SAFE? **YES NO**

BRAND:	COLOR/TRANSPARENCY/CHARACTERISTICS		
APPLICATION METHOD(S):		COATS/LAYER:	FOOD SAFE? **YES NO**

BRAND:	COLOR/TRANSPARENCY/CHARACTERISTICS		
APPLICATION METHOD(S):		COATS/LAYER:	FOOD SAFE? **YES NO**

GLAZE FIRING 1   DATE

KILN TYPE:	PROGRAM OR FIRING METHOD:	CONE:
PREHEAT/HOLD/COOL FIRING TIME/TEMP(S):		TOTAL TIME:

GLAZE/LUSTER FIRING   DATE

KILN TYPE:	PROGRAM OR FIRING METHOD:	CONE:
PREHEAT/HOLD/COOL FIRING TIME/TEMP(S):		TOTAL TIME:

NOTES:

____

____

____

____

____

SALES RECORD

SALE LOCATION:	ESTIMATED VALUE/LISTING PRICE:
SALE DATE:	TRANSACTION DETAILS:	FINAL PRICE:

PROJECT: **DATE:**

IMAGE or SKETCH

DIMENSIONS: WEIGHT:

CLAY

TYPE:	COLOR:	SOURCE:
ADDITIVE(S):		RESULTS RATING:

FORMING TECHNIQUE(S):

DECORATING TECHNIQUES & TOOLS:

DRYING TIME/NOTES:

BISQUE FIRING   DATE

KILN TYPE:	PROGRAM OR FIRING METHOD:	CONE:
PREHEAT/HOLD/COOL FIRING TIME/TEMP(S):		TOTAL TIME:
STAINS/SPRAYS/COMBUSTIBLES:		

Glaze(s)

BRAND:	COLOR/TRANSPARENCY/CHARACTERISTICS		
APPLICATION METHOD(S):		COATS/LAYER:	FOOD SAFE? **YES NO**

BRAND:	COLOR/TRANSPARENCY/CHARACTERISTICS		
APPLICATION METHOD(S):		COATS/LAYER:	FOOD SAFE? **YES NO**

BRAND:	COLOR/TRANSPARENCY/CHARACTERISTICS		
APPLICATION METHOD(S):		COATS/LAYER:	FOOD SAFE? **YES NO**

BRAND:	COLOR/TRANSPARENCY/CHARACTERISTICS		
APPLICATION METHOD(S):		COATS/LAYER:	FOOD SAFE? **YES NO**

BRAND:	COLOR/TRANSPARENCY/CHARACTERISTICS		
APPLICATION METHOD(S):		COATS/LAYER:	FOOD SAFE? **YES NO**

GLAZE FIRING 1   DATE

KILN TYPE:	PROGRAM OR FIRING METHOD:	CONE:
PREHEAT/HOLD/COOL FIRING TIME/TEMP(S):		TOTAL TIME:

GLAZE/LUSTER FIRING   DATE

KILN TYPE:	PROGRAM OR FIRING METHOD:	CONE:
PREHEAT/HOLD/COOL FIRING TIME/TEMP(S):		TOTAL TIME:

NOTES:

____

____

____

____

SALES RECORD

SALE LOCATION:	ESTIMATED VALUE/LISTING PRICE:
SALE DATE: TRANSACTION DETAILS:	FINAL PRICE:

PROJECT: **DATE:**

IMAGE or SKETCH

DIMENSIONS: **WEIGHT:**

CLAY

TYPE:	COLOR:	SOURCE:
ADDITIVE(S):		RESULTS RATING:

FORMING TECHNIQUE(S):

DECORATING TECHNIQUES & TOOLS:

DRYING TIME/NOTES:

BISQUE FIRING   DATE

KILN TYPE:	PROGRAM OR FIRING METHOD:	CONE:
PREHEAT/HOLD/COOL FIRING TIME/TEMP(S):		TOTAL TIME:
STAINS/SPRAYS/COMBUSTIBLES:		

Glaze(s)

BRAND:	COLOR/TRANSPARENCY/CHARACTERISTICS		
APPLICATION METHOD(S):		COATS/LAYER:	FOOD SAFE? **YES NO**

BRAND:	COLOR/TRANSPARENCY/CHARACTERISTICS		
APPLICATION METHOD(S):		COATS/LAYER:	FOOD SAFE? **YES NO**

BRAND:	COLOR/TRANSPARENCY/CHARACTERISTICS		
APPLICATION METHOD(S):		COATS/LAYER:	FOOD SAFE? **YES NO**

BRAND:	COLOR/TRANSPARENCY/CHARACTERISTICS		
APPLICATION METHOD(S):		COATS/LAYER:	FOOD SAFE? **YES NO**

BRAND:	COLOR/TRANSPARENCY/CHARACTERISTICS		
APPLICATION METHOD(S):		COATS/LAYER:	FOOD SAFE? **YES NO**

GLAZE FIRING 1   DATE

KILN TYPE:	PROGRAM OR FIRING METHOD:	CONE:
PREHEAT/HOLD/COOL FIRING TIME/TEMP(S):		TOTAL TIME:

GLAZE/LUSTER FIRING   DATE

KILN TYPE:	PROGRAM OR FIRING METHOD:	CONE:
PREHEAT/HOLD/COOL FIRING TIME/TEMP(S):		TOTAL TIME:

NOTES:

____

____

____

____

____

SALES RECORD

SALE LOCATION:	ESTIMATED VALUE/LISTING PRICE:	
SALE DATE:	TRANSACTION DETAILS:	FINAL PRICE:

PROJECT: DATE:

IMAGE or SKETCH

DIMENSIONS: WEIGHT:

CLAY

TYPE:	COLOR:	SOURCE:

ADDITIVE(S):	RESULTS RATING:

FORMING TECHNIQUE(S):

DECORATING TECHNIQUES & TOOLS:

DRYING TIME/NOTES:

BISQUE FIRING   DATE

KILN TYPE:	PROGRAM OR FIRING METHOD:	CONE:

PREHEAT/HOLD/COOL FIRING TIME/TEMP(S):	TOTAL TIME:

STAINS/SPRAYS/COMBUSTIBLES:

Glaze(s)

BRAND:	COLOR/TRANSPARENCY/CHARACTERISTICS		
APPLICATION METHOD(S):		COATS/LAYER:	FOOD SAFE? **YES NO**

BRAND:	COLOR/TRANSPARENCY/CHARACTERISTICS		
APPLICATION METHOD(S):		COATS/LAYER:	FOOD SAFE? **YES NO**

BRAND:	COLOR/TRANSPARENCY/CHARACTERISTICS		
APPLICATION METHOD(S):		COATS/LAYER:	FOOD SAFE? **YES NO**

BRAND:	COLOR/TRANSPARENCY/CHARACTERISTICS		
APPLICATION METHOD(S):		COATS/LAYER:	FOOD SAFE? **YES NO**

BRAND:	COLOR/TRANSPARENCY/CHARACTERISTICS		
APPLICATION METHOD(S):		COATS/LAYER:	FOOD SAFE? **YES NO**

GLAZE FIRING 1   DATE

KILN TYPE:	PROGRAM OR FIRING METHOD:	CONE:
PREHEAT/HOLD/COOL FIRING TIME/TEMP(S):		TOTAL TIME:

GLAZE/LUSTER FIRING   DATE

KILN TYPE:	PROGRAM OR FIRING METHOD:	CONE:
PREHEAT/HOLD/COOL FIRING TIME/TEMP(S):		TOTAL TIME:

NOTES:

____

____

____

____

SALES RECORD

SALE LOCATION:	ESTIMATED VALUE/LISTING PRICE:
SALE DATE: TRANSACTION DETAILS:	FINAL PRICE:

PROJECT: **DATE:**

IMAGE or SKETCH

DIMENSIONS: **WEIGHT:**

CLAY

TYPE:		COLOR:	SOURCE:	
ADDITIVE(S):				RESULTS RATING:

FORMING TECHNIQUE(S):

DECORATING TECHNIQUES & TOOLS:

DRYING TIME/NOTES:

BISQUE FIRING   DATE

KILN TYPE:	PROGRAM OR FIRING METHOD:	CONE:
PREHEAT/HOLD/COOL FIRING TIME/TEMP(S):		TOTAL TIME:
STAINS/SPRAYS/COMBUSTIBLES:		

Glaze(s)

BRAND:	COLOR/TRANSPARENCY/CHARACTERISTICS		
APPLICATION METHOD(S):		COATS/LAYER:	FOOD SAFE? **YES NO**

BRAND:	COLOR/TRANSPARENCY/CHARACTERISTICS		
APPLICATION METHOD(S):		COATS/LAYER:	FOOD SAFE? **YES NO**

BRAND:	COLOR/TRANSPARENCY/CHARACTERISTICS		
APPLICATION METHOD(S):		COATS/LAYER:	FOOD SAFE? **YES NO**

BRAND:	COLOR/TRANSPARENCY/CHARACTERISTICS		
APPLICATION METHOD(S):		COATS/LAYER:	FOOD SAFE? **YES NO**

BRAND:	COLOR/TRANSPARENCY/CHARACTERISTICS		
APPLICATION METHOD(S):		COATS/LAYER:	FOOD SAFE? **YES NO**

GLAZE FIRING 1   DATE

KILN TYPE:	PROGRAM OR FIRING METHOD:	CONE:
PREHEAT/HOLD/COOL FIRING TIME/TEMP(S):		TOTAL TIME:

GLAZE/LUSTER FIRING   DATE

KILN TYPE:	PROGRAM OR FIRING METHOD:	CONE:
PREHEAT/HOLD/COOL FIRING TIME/TEMP(S):		TOTAL TIME:

NOTES:

____

____

____

____

____

SALES RECORD

SALE LOCATION:	ESTIMATED VALUE/LISTING PRICE:
SALE DATE:	TRANSACTION DETAILS:	FINAL PRICE:

PROJECT: **DATE:**

DIMENSIONS: WEIGHT:

CLAY

TYPE:	COLOR:	SOURCE:
ADDITIVE(S):		RESULTS RATING:

FORMING TECHNIQUE(S):

DECORATING TECHNIQUES & TOOLS:

DRYING TIME/NOTES:

BISQUE FIRING   DATE

KILN TYPE:	PROGRAM OR FIRING METHOD:	CONE:
PREHEAT/HOLD/COOL FIRING TIME/TEMP(S):		TOTAL TIME:
STAINS/SPRAYS/COMBUSTIBLES:		

Glaze(s)

BRAND:	COLOR/TRANSPARENCY/CHARACTERISTICS		
APPLICATION METHOD(S):		COATS/LAYER:	FOOD SAFE? **YES NO**

BRAND:	COLOR/TRANSPARENCY/CHARACTERISTICS		
APPLICATION METHOD(S):		COATS/LAYER:	FOOD SAFE? **YES NO**

BRAND:	COLOR/TRANSPARENCY/CHARACTERISTICS		
APPLICATION METHOD(S):		COATS/LAYER:	FOOD SAFE? **YES NO**

BRAND:	COLOR/TRANSPARENCY/CHARACTERISTICS		
APPLICATION METHOD(S):		COATS/LAYER:	FOOD SAFE? **YES NO**

BRAND:	COLOR/TRANSPARENCY/CHARACTERISTICS		
APPLICATION METHOD(S):		COATS/LAYER:	FOOD SAFE? **YES NO**

GLAZE FIRING 1   DATE

KILN TYPE:	PROGRAM OR FIRING METHOD:	CONE:
PREHEAT/HOLD/COOL FIRING TIME/TEMP(S):		TOTAL TIME:

GLAZE/LUSTER FIRING   DATE

KILN TYPE:	PROGRAM OR FIRING METHOD:	CONE:
PREHEAT/HOLD/COOL FIRING TIME/TEMP(S):		TOTAL TIME:

NOTES:

____

____

____

____

____

SALES RECORD

SALE LOCATION:	ESTIMATED VALUE/LISTING PRICE:
SALE DATE:	TRANSACTION DETAILS:	FINAL PRICE:

PROJECT: ___________________________   **DATE:** ___________________________

IMAGE or SKETCH

DIMENSIONS: ___________________________   WEIGHT: ___________________________

CLAY

TYPE:	COLOR:	SOURCE:
ADDITIVE(S):		RESULTS RATING:

FORMING TECHNIQUE(S):

____

____

____

DECORATING TECHNIQUES & TOOLS:

____

____

____

DRYING TIME/NOTES:

____

____

BISQUE FIRING   DATE

KILN TYPE:	PROGRAM OR FIRING METHOD:	CONE:
PREHEAT/HOLD/COOL FIRING TIME/TEMP(S):		TOTAL TIME:
STAINS/SPRAYS/COMBUSTIBLES:		

Glaze(s)

BRAND:	COLOR/TRANSPARENCY/CHARACTERISTICS		
APPLICATION METHOD(S):		COATS/LAYER:	FOOD SAFE? **YES NO**

BRAND:	COLOR/TRANSPARENCY/CHARACTERISTICS		
APPLICATION METHOD(S):		COATS/LAYER:	FOOD SAFE? **YES NO**

BRAND:	COLOR/TRANSPARENCY/CHARACTERISTICS		
APPLICATION METHOD(S):		COATS/LAYER:	FOOD SAFE? **YES NO**

BRAND:	COLOR/TRANSPARENCY/CHARACTERISTICS		
APPLICATION METHOD(S):		COATS/LAYER:	FOOD SAFE? **YES NO**

BRAND:	COLOR/TRANSPARENCY/CHARACTERISTICS		
APPLICATION METHOD(S):		COATS/LAYER:	FOOD SAFE? **YES NO**

GLAZE FIRING 1   DATE

KILN TYPE:	PROGRAM OR FIRING METHOD:	CONE:
PREHEAT/HOLD/COOL FIRING TIME/TEMP(S):		TOTAL TIME:

GLAZE/LUSTER FIRING   DATE

KILN TYPE:	PROGRAM OR FIRING METHOD:	CONE:
PREHEAT/HOLD/COOL FIRING TIME/TEMP(S):		TOTAL TIME:

NOTES:

____

____

____

____

____

SALES RECORD

SALE LOCATION:		ESTIMATED VALUE/LISTING PRICE:
SALE DATE:	TRANSACTION DETAILS:	FINAL PRICE:

PROJECT: **DATE:**

IMAGE or SKETCH

DIMENSIONS: WEIGHT:

CLAY

TYPE:	COLOR:	SOURCE:
ADDITIVE(S):		RESULTS RATING:

FORMING TECHNIQUE(S):

DECORATING TECHNIQUES & TOOLS:

DRYING TIME/NOTES:

BISQUE FIRING   DATE

KILN TYPE:	PROGRAM OR FIRING METHOD:	CONE:
PREHEAT/HOLD/COOL FIRING TIME/TEMP(S):		TOTAL TIME:
STAINS/SPRAYS/COMBUSTIBLES:		

Glaze(s)

BRAND:	COLOR/TRANSPARENCY/CHARACTERISTICS		
APPLICATION METHOD(S):		COATS/LAYER:	FOOD SAFE? **YES NO**

BRAND:	COLOR/TRANSPARENCY/CHARACTERISTICS		
APPLICATION METHOD(S):		COATS/LAYER:	FOOD SAFE? **YES NO**

BRAND:	COLOR/TRANSPARENCY/CHARACTERISTICS		
APPLICATION METHOD(S):		COATS/LAYER:	FOOD SAFE? **YES NO**

BRAND:	COLOR/TRANSPARENCY/CHARACTERISTICS		
APPLICATION METHOD(S):		COATS/LAYER:	FOOD SAFE? **YES NO**

BRAND:	COLOR/TRANSPARENCY/CHARACTERISTICS		
APPLICATION METHOD(S):		COATS/LAYER:	FOOD SAFE? **YES NO**

GLAZE FIRING 1   DATE

KILN TYPE:	PROGRAM OR FIRING METHOD:	CONE:
PREHEAT/HOLD/COOL FIRING TIME/TEMP(S):		TOTAL TIME:

GLAZE/LUSTER FIRING   DATE

KILN TYPE:	PROGRAM OR FIRING METHOD:	CONE:
PREHEAT/HOLD/COOL FIRING TIME/TEMP(S):		TOTAL TIME:

NOTES:

____

____

____

____

____

SALES RECORD

SALE LOCATION:	ESTIMATED VALUE/LISTING PRICE:
SALE DATE:	TRANSACTION DETAILS:	FINAL PRICE:

PROJECT: **DATE:**

IMAGE or SKETCH

DIMENSIONS: WEIGHT:

CLAY

TYPE:	COLOR:	SOURCE:

ADDITIVE(S):	RESULTS RATING:

FORMING TECHNIQUE(S):

DECORATING TECHNIQUES & TOOLS:

DRYING TIME/NOTES:

BISQUE FIRING   DATE

KILN TYPE:	PROGRAM OR FIRING METHOD:	CONE:

PREHEAT/HOLD/COOL FIRING TIME/TEMP(S):	TOTAL TIME:

STAINS/SPRAYS/COMBUSTIBLES:

Glaze(s)

BRAND:	COLOR/TRANSPARENCY/CHARACTERISTICS		
APPLICATION METHOD(S):		COATS/LAYER:	FOOD SAFE? **YES NO**

BRAND:	COLOR/TRANSPARENCY/CHARACTERISTICS		
APPLICATION METHOD(S):		COATS/LAYER:	FOOD SAFE? **YES NO**

BRAND:	COLOR/TRANSPARENCY/CHARACTERISTICS		
APPLICATION METHOD(S):		COATS/LAYER:	FOOD SAFE? **YES NO**

BRAND:	COLOR/TRANSPARENCY/CHARACTERISTICS		
APPLICATION METHOD(S):		COATS/LAYER:	FOOD SAFE? **YES NO**

BRAND:	COLOR/TRANSPARENCY/CHARACTERISTICS		
APPLICATION METHOD(S):		COATS/LAYER:	FOOD SAFE? **YES NO**

GLAZE FIRING 1   DATE

KILN TYPE:	PROGRAM OR FIRING METHOD:	CONE:
PREHEAT/HOLD/COOL FIRING TIME/TEMP(S):		TOTAL TIME:

GLAZE/LUSTER FIRING   DATE

KILN TYPE:	PROGRAM OR FIRING METHOD:	CONE:
PREHEAT/HOLD/COOL FIRING TIME/TEMP(S):		TOTAL TIME:

NOTES:

____

____

____

____

SALES RECORD

SALE LOCATION:		ESTIMATED VALUE/LISTING PRICE:
SALE DATE:	TRANSACTION DETAILS:	FINAL PRICE:

PROJECT: ___________________________   **DATE:** ___________________________

IMAGE or SKETCH

DIMENSIONS: ___________________________   WEIGHT: ___________________________

CLAY

TYPE:	COLOR:	SOURCE:

ADDITIVE(S):	RESULTS RATING:
	⚱ ⚱ ⚱ ⚱ ⚱

FORMING TECHNIQUE(S):

____

____

____

DECORATING TECHNIQUES & TOOLS:

____

____

____

DRYING TIME/NOTES:

____

____

BISQUE FIRING   DATE

KILN TYPE:	PROGRAM OR FIRING METHOD:	CONE:

PREHEAT/HOLD/COOL FIRING TIME/TEMP(S):	TOTAL TIME:

STAINS/SPRAYS/COMBUSTIBLES:

Glaze(s)

BRAND:	COLOR/TRANSPARENCY/CHARACTERISTICS		
APPLICATION METHOD(S):		COATS/LAYER:	FOOD SAFE? **YES NO**

BRAND:	COLOR/TRANSPARENCY/CHARACTERISTICS		
APPLICATION METHOD(S):		COATS/LAYER:	FOOD SAFE? **YES NO**

BRAND:	COLOR/TRANSPARENCY/CHARACTERISTICS		
APPLICATION METHOD(S):		COATS/LAYER:	FOOD SAFE? **YES NO**

BRAND:	COLOR/TRANSPARENCY/CHARACTERISTICS		
APPLICATION METHOD(S):		COATS/LAYER:	FOOD SAFE? **YES NO**

BRAND:	COLOR/TRANSPARENCY/CHARACTERISTICS		
APPLICATION METHOD(S):		COATS/LAYER:	FOOD SAFE? **YES NO**

GLAZE FIRING 1   DATE

KILN TYPE:	PROGRAM OR FIRING METHOD:	CONE:
PREHEAT/HOLD/COOL FIRING TIME/TEMP(S):		TOTAL TIME:

GLAZE/LUSTER FIRING   DATE

KILN TYPE:	PROGRAM OR FIRING METHOD:	CONE:
PREHEAT/HOLD/COOL FIRING TIME/TEMP(S):		TOTAL TIME:

NOTES:

____

____

____

____

____

SALES RECORD

SALE LOCATION:	ESTIMATED VALUE/LISTING PRICE:
SALE DATE:	TRANSACTION DETAILS:	FINAL PRICE:

PROJECT: ____

DATE: ___________________________

IMAGE or SKETCH

DIMENSIONS: _____________________________________

WEIGHT: ___________________________

CLAY

TYPE:	COLOR:	SOURCE:
ADDITIVE(S):		RESULTS RATING:

FORMING TECHNIQUE(S):

DECORATING TECHNIQUES & TOOLS:

DRYING TIME/NOTES:

BISQUE FIRING   DATE

KILN TYPE:	PROGRAM OR FIRING METHOD:	CONE:
PREHEAT/HOLD/COOL FIRING TIME/TEMP(S):		TOTAL TIME:
STAINS/SPRAYS/COMBUSTIBLES:		

Glaze(s)

BRAND:	COLOR/TRANSPARENCY/CHARACTERISTICS		
APPLICATION METHOD(S):		COATS/LAYER:	FOOD SAFE? **YES NO**

BRAND:	COLOR/TRANSPARENCY/CHARACTERISTICS		
APPLICATION METHOD(S):		COATS/LAYER:	FOOD SAFE? **YES NO**

BRAND:	COLOR/TRANSPARENCY/CHARACTERISTICS		
APPLICATION METHOD(S):		COATS/LAYER:	FOOD SAFE? **YES NO**

BRAND:	COLOR/TRANSPARENCY/CHARACTERISTICS		
APPLICATION METHOD(S):		COATS/LAYER:	FOOD SAFE? **YES NO**

BRAND:	COLOR/TRANSPARENCY/CHARACTERISTICS		
APPLICATION METHOD(S):		COATS/LAYER:	FOOD SAFE? **YES NO**

GLAZE FIRING 1   DATE

KILN TYPE:	PROGRAM OR FIRING METHOD:	CONE:
PREHEAT/HOLD/COOL FIRING TIME/TEMP(S):		TOTAL TIME:

GLAZE/LUSTER FIRING   DATE

KILN TYPE:	PROGRAM OR FIRING METHOD:	CONE:
PREHEAT/HOLD/COOL FIRING TIME/TEMP(S):		TOTAL TIME:

NOTES:

____

____

____

____

____

SALES RECORD

SALE LOCATION:	ESTIMATED VALUE/LISTING PRICE:
SALE DATE:	TRANSACTION DETAILS:	FINAL PRICE:

PROJECT: **DATE:**

DIMENSIONS: WEIGHT:

CLAY

TYPE:	COLOR:	SOURCE:
ADDITIVE(S):		RESULTS RATING:

FORMING TECHNIQUE(S):

DECORATING TECHNIQUES & TOOLS:

DRYING TIME/NOTES:

BISQUE FIRING   DATE

KILN TYPE:	PROGRAM OR FIRING METHOD:	CONE:
PREHEAT/HOLD/COOL FIRING TIME/TEMP(S):		TOTAL TIME:
STAINS/SPRAYS/COMBUSTIBLES:		

Glaze(s)

BRAND:	COLOR/TRANSPARENCY/CHARACTERISTICS		
APPLICATION METHOD(S):		COATS/LAYER:	FOOD SAFE? **YES NO**

BRAND:	COLOR/TRANSPARENCY/CHARACTERISTICS		
APPLICATION METHOD(S):		COATS/LAYER:	FOOD SAFE? **YES NO**

BRAND:	COLOR/TRANSPARENCY/CHARACTERISTICS		
APPLICATION METHOD(S):		COATS/LAYER:	FOOD SAFE? **YES NO**

BRAND:	COLOR/TRANSPARENCY/CHARACTERISTICS		
APPLICATION METHOD(S):		COATS/LAYER:	FOOD SAFE? **YES NO**

BRAND:	COLOR/TRANSPARENCY/CHARACTERISTICS		
APPLICATION METHOD(S):		COATS/LAYER:	FOOD SAFE? **YES NO**

GLAZE FIRING 1   DATE

KILN TYPE:	PROGRAM OR FIRING METHOD:	CONE:
PREHEAT/HOLD/COOL FIRING TIME/TEMP(S):		TOTAL TIME:

GLAZE/LUSTER FIRING   DATE

KILN TYPE:	PROGRAM OR FIRING METHOD:	CONE:
PREHEAT/HOLD/COOL FIRING TIME/TEMP(S):		TOTAL TIME:

NOTES:

____

____

____

____

____

SALES RECORD

SALE LOCATION:	ESTIMATED VALUE/LISTING PRICE:	
SALE DATE:	TRANSACTION DETAILS:	FINAL PRICE:

PROJECT: **DATE:**

IMAGE or SKETCH

DIMENSIONS: **WEIGHT:**

CLAY

TYPE:		COLOR:	SOURCE:	
ADDITIVE(S):				RESULTS RATING:

FORMING TECHNIQUE(S):

DECORATING TECHNIQUES & TOOLS:

DRYING TIME/NOTES:

BISQUE FIRING   DATE

KILN TYPE:	PROGRAM OR FIRING METHOD:	CONE:
PREHEAT/HOLD/COOL FIRING TIME/TEMP(S):		TOTAL TIME:
STAINS/SPRAYS/COMBUSTIBLES:		

Glaze(s)

BRAND:	COLOR/TRANSPARENCY/CHARACTERISTICS		
APPLICATION METHOD(S):		COATS/LAYER:	FOOD SAFE? **YES NO**

BRAND:	COLOR/TRANSPARENCY/CHARACTERISTICS		
APPLICATION METHOD(S):		COATS/LAYER:	FOOD SAFE? **YES NO**

BRAND:	COLOR/TRANSPARENCY/CHARACTERISTICS		
APPLICATION METHOD(S):		COATS/LAYER:	FOOD SAFE? **YES NO**

BRAND:	COLOR/TRANSPARENCY/CHARACTERISTICS		
APPLICATION METHOD(S):		COATS/LAYER:	FOOD SAFE? **YES NO**

BRAND:	COLOR/TRANSPARENCY/CHARACTERISTICS		
APPLICATION METHOD(S):		COATS/LAYER:	FOOD SAFE? **YES NO**

GLAZE FIRING 1   DATE

KILN TYPE:	PROGRAM OR FIRING METHOD:	CONE:
PREHEAT/HOLD/COOL FIRING TIME/TEMP(S):		TOTAL TIME:

GLAZE/LUSTER FIRING   DATE

KILN TYPE:	PROGRAM OR FIRING METHOD:	CONE:
PREHEAT/HOLD/COOL FIRING TIME/TEMP(S):		TOTAL TIME:

NOTES:

____

____

____

____

____

SALES RECORD

SALE LOCATION:	ESTIMATED VALUE/LISTING PRICE:
SALE DATE:	TRANSACTION DETAILS:	FINAL PRICE:

PROJECT: **DATE:**

DIMENSIONS: WEIGHT:

CLAY

TYPE:	COLOR:	SOURCE:
ADDITIVE(S):		RESULTS RATING:

FORMING TECHNIQUE(S):

____

____

DECORATING TECHNIQUES & TOOLS:

____

____

DRYING TIME/NOTES:

____

BISQUE FIRING   DATE

KILN TYPE:	PROGRAM OR FIRING METHOD:	CONE:
PREHEAT/HOLD/COOL FIRING TIME/TEMP(S):		TOTAL TIME:
STAINS/SPRAYS/COMBUSTIBLES:		

Glaze(s)

BRAND:	COLOR/TRANSPARENCY/CHARACTERISTICS		
APPLICATION METHOD(S):		COATS/LAYER:	FOOD SAFE? **YES NO**

BRAND:	COLOR/TRANSPARENCY/CHARACTERISTICS		
APPLICATION METHOD(S):		COATS/LAYER:	FOOD SAFE? **YES NO**

BRAND:	COLOR/TRANSPARENCY/CHARACTERISTICS		
APPLICATION METHOD(S):		COATS/LAYER:	FOOD SAFE? **YES NO**

BRAND:	COLOR/TRANSPARENCY/CHARACTERISTICS		
APPLICATION METHOD(S):		COATS/LAYER:	FOOD SAFE? **YES NO**

BRAND:	COLOR/TRANSPARENCY/CHARACTERISTICS		
APPLICATION METHOD(S):		COATS/LAYER:	FOOD SAFE? **YES NO**

GLAZE FIRING 1   DATE

KILN TYPE:	PROGRAM OR FIRING METHOD:	CONE:
PREHEAT/HOLD/COOL FIRING TIME/TEMP(S):		TOTAL TIME:

GLAZE/LUSTER FIRING   DATE

KILN TYPE:	PROGRAM OR FIRING METHOD:	CONE:
PREHEAT/HOLD/COOL FIRING TIME/TEMP(S):		TOTAL TIME:

NOTES:

____

____

____

____

SALES RECORD

SALE LOCATION:	ESTIMATED VALUE/LISTING PRICE:
SALE DATE:	TRANSACTION DETAILS:	FINAL PRICE:

PROJECT: **DATE:**

IMAGE or SKETCH

DIMENSIONS: WEIGHT:

CLAY

TYPE:	COLOR:	SOURCE:
ADDITIVE(S):		RESULTS RATING:

FORMING TECHNIQUE(S):

DECORATING TECHNIQUES & TOOLS:

DRYING TIME/NOTES:

BISQUE FIRING   DATE

KILN TYPE:	PROGRAM OR FIRING METHOD:	CONE:
PREHEAT/HOLD/COOL FIRING TIME/TEMP(S):		TOTAL TIME:
STAINS/SPRAYS/COMBUSTIBLES:		

Glaze(s)

BRAND:	COLOR/TRANSPARENCY/CHARACTERISTICS		
APPLICATION METHOD(S):		COATS/LAYER:	FOOD SAFE? **YES NO**

BRAND:	COLOR/TRANSPARENCY/CHARACTERISTICS		
APPLICATION METHOD(S):		COATS/LAYER:	FOOD SAFE? **YES NO**

BRAND:	COLOR/TRANSPARENCY/CHARACTERISTICS		
APPLICATION METHOD(S):		COATS/LAYER:	FOOD SAFE? **YES NO**

BRAND:	COLOR/TRANSPARENCY/CHARACTERISTICS		
APPLICATION METHOD(S):		COATS/LAYER:	FOOD SAFE? **YES NO**

BRAND:	COLOR/TRANSPARENCY/CHARACTERISTICS		
APPLICATION METHOD(S):		COATS/LAYER:	FOOD SAFE? **YES NO**

GLAZE FIRING 1   DATE

KILN TYPE:	PROGRAM OR FIRING METHOD:	CONE:
PREHEAT/HOLD/COOL FIRING TIME/TEMP(S):		TOTAL TIME:

GLAZE/LUSTER FIRING   DATE

KILN TYPE:	PROGRAM OR FIRING METHOD:	CONE:
PREHEAT/HOLD/COOL FIRING TIME/TEMP(S):		TOTAL TIME:

NOTES:

____

____

____

____

____

SALES RECORD

SALE LOCATION:	ESTIMATED VALUE/LISTING PRICE:
SALE DATE: TRANSACTION DETAILS:	FINAL PRICE:

PROJECT: **DATE:**

IMAGE or SKETCH

DIMENSIONS: **WEIGHT:**

CLAY

TYPE:	COLOR:	SOURCE:
ADDITIVE(S):		RESULTS RATING:

FORMING TECHNIQUE(S):

DECORATING TECHNIQUES & TOOLS:

DRYING TIME/NOTES:

BISQUE FIRING   DATE

KILN TYPE:	PROGRAM OR FIRING METHOD:	CONE:
PREHEAT/HOLD/COOL FIRING TIME/TEMP(S):		TOTAL TIME:
STAINS/SPRAYS/COMBUSTIBLES:		

Glaze(s)

BRAND:	COLOR/TRANSPARENCY/CHARACTERISTICS		
APPLICATION METHOD(S):		COATS/LAYER:	FOOD SAFE? **YES NO**

BRAND:	COLOR/TRANSPARENCY/CHARACTERISTICS		
APPLICATION METHOD(S):		COATS/LAYER:	FOOD SAFE? **YES NO**

BRAND:	COLOR/TRANSPARENCY/CHARACTERISTICS		
APPLICATION METHOD(S):		COATS/LAYER:	FOOD SAFE? **YES NO**

BRAND:	COLOR/TRANSPARENCY/CHARACTERISTICS		
APPLICATION METHOD(S):		COATS/LAYER:	FOOD SAFE? **YES NO**

BRAND:	COLOR/TRANSPARENCY/CHARACTERISTICS		
APPLICATION METHOD(S):		COATS/LAYER:	FOOD SAFE? **YES NO**

GLAZE FIRING 1   DATE

KILN TYPE:	PROGRAM OR FIRING METHOD:	CONE:
PREHEAT/HOLD/COOL FIRING TIME/TEMP(S):		TOTAL TIME:

GLAZE/LUSTER FIRING   DATE

KILN TYPE:	PROGRAM OR FIRING METHOD:	CONE:
PREHEAT/HOLD/COOL FIRING TIME/TEMP(S):		TOTAL TIME:

NOTES:

____

____

____

____

____

SALES RECORD

SALE LOCATION:	ESTIMATED VALUE/LISTING PRICE:
SALE DATE:	TRANSACTION DETAILS:	FINAL PRICE:

PROJECT: **DATE:**

IMAGE or SKETCH

DIMENSIONS: **WEIGHT:**

CLAY

TYPE:	COLOR:	SOURCE:
ADDITIVE(S):		RESULTS RATING:

FORMING TECHNIQUE(S):

DECORATING TECHNIQUES & TOOLS:

DRYING TIME/NOTES:

BISQUE FIRING   DATE

KILN TYPE:	PROGRAM OR FIRING METHOD:	CONE:
PREHEAT/HOLD/COOL FIRING TIME/TEMP(S):		TOTAL TIME:
STAINS/SPRAYS/COMBUSTIBLES:		

Glaze(s)

BRAND:	COLOR/TRANSPARENCY/CHARACTERISTICS		
APPLICATION METHOD(S):		COATS/LAYER:	FOOD SAFE? **YES NO**

BRAND:	COLOR/TRANSPARENCY/CHARACTERISTICS		
APPLICATION METHOD(S):		COATS/LAYER:	FOOD SAFE? **YES NO**

BRAND:	COLOR/TRANSPARENCY/CHARACTERISTICS		
APPLICATION METHOD(S):		COATS/LAYER:	FOOD SAFE? **YES NO**

BRAND:	COLOR/TRANSPARENCY/CHARACTERISTICS		
APPLICATION METHOD(S):		COATS/LAYER:	FOOD SAFE? **YES NO**

BRAND:	COLOR/TRANSPARENCY/CHARACTERISTICS		
APPLICATION METHOD(S):		COATS/LAYER:	FOOD SAFE? **YES NO**

GLAZE FIRING 1   DATE

KILN TYPE:	PROGRAM OR FIRING METHOD:	CONE:
PREHEAT/HOLD/COOL FIRING TIME/TEMP(S):		TOTAL TIME:

GLAZE/LUSTER FIRING   DATE

KILN TYPE:	PROGRAM OR FIRING METHOD:	CONE:
PREHEAT/HOLD/COOL FIRING TIME/TEMP(S):		TOTAL TIME:

NOTES:

____

____

____

____

____

SALES RECORD

SALE LOCATION:	ESTIMATED VALUE/LISTING PRICE:
SALE DATE:	TRANSACTION DETAILS:	FINAL PRICE:

PROJECT: **DATE:**

IMAGE or SKETCH

DIMENSIONS: WEIGHT:

CLAY

TYPE:		COLOR:	SOURCE:	
ADDITIVE(S):				RESULTS RATING:

FORMING TECHNIQUE(S):

DECORATING TECHNIQUES & TOOLS:

DRYING TIME/NOTES:

BISQUE FIRING   DATE

KILN TYPE:	PROGRAM OR FIRING METHOD:	CONE:
PREHEAT/HOLD/COOL FIRING TIME/TEMP(S):		TOTAL TIME:
STAINS/SPRAYS/COMBUSTIBLES:		

Glaze(s)

BRAND:	COLOR/TRANSPARENCY/CHARACTERISTICS		
APPLICATION METHOD(S):		COATS/LAYER:	FOOD SAFE? **YES NO**

BRAND:	COLOR/TRANSPARENCY/CHARACTERISTICS		
APPLICATION METHOD(S):		COATS/LAYER:	FOOD SAFE? **YES NO**

BRAND:	COLOR/TRANSPARENCY/CHARACTERISTICS		
APPLICATION METHOD(S):		COATS/LAYER:	FOOD SAFE? **YES NO**

BRAND:	COLOR/TRANSPARENCY/CHARACTERISTICS		
APPLICATION METHOD(S):		COATS/LAYER:	FOOD SAFE? **YES NO**

BRAND:	COLOR/TRANSPARENCY/CHARACTERISTICS		
APPLICATION METHOD(S):		COATS/LAYER:	FOOD SAFE? **YES NO**

GLAZE FIRING 1   DATE

KILN TYPE:	PROGRAM OR FIRING METHOD:	CONE:
PREHEAT/HOLD/COOL FIRING TIME/TEMP(S):		TOTAL TIME:

GLAZE/LUSTER FIRING   DATE

KILN TYPE:	PROGRAM OR FIRING METHOD:	CONE:
PREHEAT/HOLD/COOL FIRING TIME/TEMP(S):		TOTAL TIME:

NOTES:

____

____

____

____

____

SALES RECORD

SALE LOCATION:	ESTIMATED VALUE/LISTING PRICE:
SALE DATE:	TRANSACTION DETAILS:		FINAL PRICE:

PROJECT: **DATE:**

IMAGE or SKETCH

DIMENSIONS: **WEIGHT:**

CLAY

TYPE:	COLOR:	SOURCE:
ADDITIVE(S):		RESULTS RATING:

FORMING TECHNIQUE(S):

DECORATING TECHNIQUES & TOOLS:

DRYING TIME/NOTES:

BISQUE FIRING   DATE

KILN TYPE:	PROGRAM OR FIRING METHOD:	CONE:
PREHEAT/HOLD/COOL FIRING TIME/TEMP(S):		TOTAL TIME:
STAINS/SPRAYS/COMBUSTIBLES:		

Glaze(s)

BRAND:	COLOR/TRANSPARENCY/CHARACTERISTICS		
APPLICATION METHOD(S):		COATS/LAYER:	FOOD SAFE? **YES NO**

BRAND:	COLOR/TRANSPARENCY/CHARACTERISTICS		
APPLICATION METHOD(S):		COATS/LAYER:	FOOD SAFE? **YES NO**

BRAND:	COLOR/TRANSPARENCY/CHARACTERISTICS		
APPLICATION METHOD(S):		COATS/LAYER:	FOOD SAFE? **YES NO**

BRAND:	COLOR/TRANSPARENCY/CHARACTERISTICS		
APPLICATION METHOD(S):		COATS/LAYER:	FOOD SAFE? **YES NO**

BRAND:	COLOR/TRANSPARENCY/CHARACTERISTICS		
APPLICATION METHOD(S):		COATS/LAYER:	FOOD SAFE? **YES NO**

GLAZE FIRING 1   DATE

KILN TYPE:	PROGRAM OR FIRING METHOD:	CONE:
PREHEAT/HOLD/COOL FIRING TIME/TEMP(S):		TOTAL TIME:

GLAZE/LUSTER FIRING   DATE

KILN TYPE:	PROGRAM OR FIRING METHOD:	CONE:
PREHEAT/HOLD/COOL FIRING TIME/TEMP(S):		TOTAL TIME:

NOTES:

____

____

____

____

____

SALES RECORD

SALE LOCATION:	ESTIMATED VALUE/LISTING PRICE:
SALE DATE:	TRANSACTION DETAILS:	FINAL PRICE:

PROJECT: DATE:

IMAGE or SKETCH

DIMENSIONS: WEIGHT:

CLAY

TYPE:	COLOR:	SOURCE:
ADDITIVE(S):		RESULTS RATING:

FORMING TECHNIQUE(S):

DECORATING TECHNIQUES & TOOLS:

DRYING TIME/NOTES:

BISQUE FIRING   DATE

KILN TYPE:	PROGRAM OR FIRING METHOD:	CONE:
PREHEAT/HOLD/COOL FIRING TIME/TEMP(S):		TOTAL TIME:
STAINS/SPRAYS/COMBUSTIBLES:		

Glaze(s)

BRAND:	COLOR/TRANSPARENCY/CHARACTERISTICS		
APPLICATION METHOD(S):		COATS/LAYER:	FOOD SAFE? **YES NO**

BRAND:	COLOR/TRANSPARENCY/CHARACTERISTICS		
APPLICATION METHOD(S):		COATS/LAYER:	FOOD SAFE? **YES NO**

BRAND:	COLOR/TRANSPARENCY/CHARACTERISTICS		
APPLICATION METHOD(S):		COATS/LAYER:	FOOD SAFE? **YES NO**

BRAND:	COLOR/TRANSPARENCY/CHARACTERISTICS		
APPLICATION METHOD(S):		COATS/LAYER:	FOOD SAFE? **YES NO**

BRAND:	COLOR/TRANSPARENCY/CHARACTERISTICS		
APPLICATION METHOD(S):		COATS/LAYER:	FOOD SAFE? **YES NO**

GLAZE FIRING 1   DATE

KILN TYPE:	PROGRAM OR FIRING METHOD:	CONE:
PREHEAT/HOLD/COOL FIRING TIME/TEMP(S):		TOTAL TIME:

GLAZE/LUSTER FIRING   DATE

KILN TYPE:	PROGRAM OR FIRING METHOD:	CONE:
PREHEAT/HOLD/COOL FIRING TIME/TEMP(S):		TOTAL TIME:

NOTES:

____

____

____

____

____

SALES RECORD

SALE LOCATION:		ESTIMATED VALUE/LISTING PRICE:
SALE DATE:	TRANSACTION DETAILS:	FINAL PRICE:

PROJECT: **DATE:**

IMAGE or SKETCH

DIMENSIONS: WEIGHT:

CLAY

TYPE:	COLOR:	SOURCE:
ADDITIVE(S):		RESULTS RATING:

FORMING TECHNIQUE(S):

DECORATING TECHNIQUES & TOOLS:

DRYING TIME/NOTES:

BISQUE FIRING   DATE

KILN TYPE:	PROGRAM OR FIRING METHOD:	CONE:
PREHEAT/HOLD/COOL FIRING TIME/TEMP(S):		TOTAL TIME:
STAINS/SPRAYS/COMBUSTIBLES:		

Glaze(s)

<table>
<tr><td>BRAND:</td><td colspan="3">COLOR/TRANSPARENCY/CHARACTERISTICS</td></tr>
<tr><td>APPLICATION METHOD(S):</td><td>COATS/LAYER:</td><td colspan="2">FOOD SAFE?
YES NO</td></tr>
</table>

<table>
<tr><td>BRAND:</td><td colspan="3">COLOR/TRANSPARENCY/CHARACTERISTICS</td></tr>
<tr><td>APPLICATION METHOD(S):</td><td>COATS/LAYER:</td><td colspan="2">FOOD SAFE?
YES NO</td></tr>
</table>

<table>
<tr><td>BRAND:</td><td colspan="3">COLOR/TRANSPARENCY/CHARACTERISTICS</td></tr>
<tr><td>APPLICATION METHOD(S):</td><td>COATS/LAYER:</td><td colspan="2">FOOD SAFE?
YES NO</td></tr>
</table>

<table>
<tr><td>BRAND:</td><td colspan="3">COLOR/TRANSPARENCY/CHARACTERISTICS</td></tr>
<tr><td>APPLICATION METHOD(S):</td><td>COATS/LAYER:</td><td colspan="2">FOOD SAFE?
YES NO</td></tr>
</table>

<table>
<tr><td>BRAND:</td><td colspan="3">COLOR/TRANSPARENCY/CHARACTERISTICS</td></tr>
<tr><td>APPLICATION METHOD(S):</td><td>COATS/LAYER:</td><td colspan="2">FOOD SAFE?
YES NO</td></tr>
</table>

GLAZE FIRING 1   DATE

<table>
<tr><td>KILN TYPE:</td><td>PROGRAM OR FIRING METHOD:</td><td>CONE:</td></tr>
<tr><td colspan="2">PREHEAT/HOLD/COOL FIRING TIME/TEMP(S):</td><td>TOTAL TIME:</td></tr>
</table>

GLAZE/LUSTER FIRING   DATE

<table>
<tr><td>KILN TYPE:</td><td>PROGRAM OR FIRING METHOD:</td><td>CONE:</td></tr>
<tr><td colspan="2">PREHEAT/HOLD/COOL FIRING TIME/TEMP(S):</td><td>TOTAL TIME:</td></tr>
</table>

NOTES:

____

____

____

____

____

SALES RECORD

<table>
<tr><td>SALE LOCATION:</td><td>ESTIMATED VALUE/LISTING PRICE:</td></tr>
<tr><td>SALE DATE:</td><td>TRANSACTION DETAILS:</td><td>FINAL PRICE:</td></tr>
</table>

PROJECT: **DATE:**

IMAGE or SKETCH

DIMENSIONS: WEIGHT:

CLAY

TYPE:		COLOR:	SOURCE:	
ADDITIVE(S):				RESULTS RATING:

FORMING TECHNIQUE(S):

DECORATING TECHNIQUES & TOOLS:

DRYING TIME/NOTES:

BISQUE FIRING   DATE

KILN TYPE:	PROGRAM OR FIRING METHOD:	CONE:
PREHEAT/HOLD/COOL FIRING TIME/TEMP(S):		TOTAL TIME:
STAINS/SPRAYS/COMBUSTIBLES:		

Glaze(s)

BRAND:	COLOR/TRANSPARENCY/CHARACTERISTICS		
APPLICATION METHOD(S):		COATS/LAYER:	FOOD SAFE? **YES NO**

BRAND:	COLOR/TRANSPARENCY/CHARACTERISTICS		
APPLICATION METHOD(S):		COATS/LAYER:	FOOD SAFE? **YES NO**

BRAND:	COLOR/TRANSPARENCY/CHARACTERISTICS		
APPLICATION METHOD(S):		COATS/LAYER:	FOOD SAFE? **YES NO**

BRAND:	COLOR/TRANSPARENCY/CHARACTERISTICS		
APPLICATION METHOD(S):		COATS/LAYER:	FOOD SAFE? **YES NO**

BRAND:	COLOR/TRANSPARENCY/CHARACTERISTICS		
APPLICATION METHOD(S):		COATS/LAYER:	FOOD SAFE? **YES NO**

GLAZE FIRING 1   DATE

KILN TYPE:	PROGRAM OR FIRING METHOD:	CONE:
PREHEAT/HOLD/COOL FIRING TIME/TEMP(S):		TOTAL TIME:

GLAZE/LUSTER FIRING   DATE

KILN TYPE:	PROGRAM OR FIRING METHOD:	CONE:
PREHEAT/HOLD/COOL FIRING TIME/TEMP(S):		TOTAL TIME:

NOTES:

____

____

____

____

____

SALES RECORD

SALE LOCATION:	ESTIMATED VALUE/LISTING PRICE:

SALE DATE:	TRANSACTION DETAILS:	FINAL PRICE:

PROJECT: **DATE:**

IMAGE or SKETCH

DIMENSIONS: **WEIGHT:**

CLAY

TYPE:	COLOR:	SOURCE:	
ADDITIVE(S):			RESULTS RATING:

FORMING TECHNIQUE(S):

DECORATING TECHNIQUES & TOOLS:

DRYING TIME/NOTES:

BISQUE FIRING   DATE

KILN TYPE:	PROGRAM OR FIRING METHOD:	CONE:
PREHEAT/HOLD/COOL FIRING TIME/TEMP(S):		TOTAL TIME:
STAINS/SPRAYS/COMBUSTIBLES:		

Glaze(s)

BRAND:	COLOR/TRANSPARENCY/CHARACTERISTICS		
APPLICATION METHOD(S):		COATS/LAYER:	FOOD SAFE? **YES NO**

BRAND:	COLOR/TRANSPARENCY/CHARACTERISTICS		
APPLICATION METHOD(S):		COATS/LAYER:	FOOD SAFE? **YES NO**

BRAND:	COLOR/TRANSPARENCY/CHARACTERISTICS		
APPLICATION METHOD(S):		COATS/LAYER:	FOOD SAFE? **YES NO**

BRAND:	COLOR/TRANSPARENCY/CHARACTERISTICS		
APPLICATION METHOD(S):		COATS/LAYER:	FOOD SAFE? **YES NO**

BRAND:	COLOR/TRANSPARENCY/CHARACTERISTICS		
APPLICATION METHOD(S):		COATS/LAYER:	FOOD SAFE? **YES NO**

GLAZE FIRING 1   DATE

KILN TYPE:	PROGRAM OR FIRING METHOD:	CONE:
PREHEAT/HOLD/COOL FIRING TIME/TEMP(S):		TOTAL TIME:

GLAZE/LUSTER FIRING   DATE

KILN TYPE:	PROGRAM OR FIRING METHOD:	CONE:
PREHEAT/HOLD/COOL FIRING TIME/TEMP(S):		TOTAL TIME:

NOTES:

____

____

____

____

____

SALES RECORD

SALE LOCATION:	ESTIMATED VALUE/LISTING PRICE:	
SALE DATE:	TRANSACTION DETAILS:	FINAL PRICE:

PROJECT: **DATE:**

IMAGE or SKETCH

DIMENSIONS: WEIGHT:

CLAY

TYPE:	COLOR:	SOURCE:
ADDITIVE(S):		RESULTS RATING:

FORMING TECHNIQUE(S):

DECORATING TECHNIQUES & TOOLS:

DRYING TIME/NOTES:

BISQUE FIRING   DATE

KILN TYPE:	PROGRAM OR FIRING METHOD:	CONE:
PREHEAT/HOLD/COOL FIRING TIME/TEMP(S):		TOTAL TIME:
STAINS/SPRAYS/COMBUSTIBLES:		

Glaze(s)

BRAND:	COLOR/TRANSPARENCY/CHARACTERISTICS		
APPLICATION METHOD(S):		COATS/LAYER:	FOOD SAFE? **YES NO**

BRAND:	COLOR/TRANSPARENCY/CHARACTERISTICS		
APPLICATION METHOD(S):		COATS/LAYER:	FOOD SAFE? **YES NO**

BRAND:	COLOR/TRANSPARENCY/CHARACTERISTICS		
APPLICATION METHOD(S):		COATS/LAYER:	FOOD SAFE? **YES NO**

BRAND:	COLOR/TRANSPARENCY/CHARACTERISTICS		
APPLICATION METHOD(S):		COATS/LAYER:	FOOD SAFE? **YES NO**

BRAND:	COLOR/TRANSPARENCY/CHARACTERISTICS		
APPLICATION METHOD(S):		COATS/LAYER:	FOOD SAFE? **YES NO**

GLAZE FIRING 1   DATE

KILN TYPE:	PROGRAM OR FIRING METHOD:	CONE:
PREHEAT/HOLD/COOL FIRING TIME/TEMP(S):		TOTAL TIME:

GLAZE/LUSTER FIRING   DATE

KILN TYPE:	PROGRAM OR FIRING METHOD:	CONE:
PREHEAT/HOLD/COOL FIRING TIME/TEMP(S):		TOTAL TIME:

NOTES:

____

____

____

____

____

SALES RECORD

SALE LOCATION:	ESTIMATED VALUE/LISTING PRICE:
SALE DATE: TRANSACTION DETAILS:	FINAL PRICE:

PROJECT: **DATE:**

IMAGE or SKETCH

DIMENSIONS: **WEIGHT:**

CLAY

TYPE:	COLOR:	SOURCE:
ADDITIVE(S):		RESULTS RATING:

FORMING TECHNIQUE(S):

DECORATING TECHNIQUES & TOOLS:

DRYING TIME/NOTES:

BISQUE FIRING   DATE

KILN TYPE:	PROGRAM OR FIRING METHOD:	CONE:
PREHEAT/HOLD/COOL FIRING TIME/TEMP(S):		TOTAL TIME:
STAINS/SPRAYS/COMBUSTIBLES:		

Glaze(s)

BRAND:	COLOR/TRANSPARENCY/CHARACTERISTICS		
APPLICATION METHOD(S):		COATS/LAYER:	FOOD SAFE? **YES NO**

BRAND:	COLOR/TRANSPARENCY/CHARACTERISTICS		
APPLICATION METHOD(S):		COATS/LAYER:	FOOD SAFE? **YES NO**

BRAND:	COLOR/TRANSPARENCY/CHARACTERISTICS		
APPLICATION METHOD(S):		COATS/LAYER:	FOOD SAFE? **YES NO**

BRAND:	COLOR/TRANSPARENCY/CHARACTERISTICS		
APPLICATION METHOD(S):		COATS/LAYER:	FOOD SAFE? **YES NO**

BRAND:	COLOR/TRANSPARENCY/CHARACTERISTICS		
APPLICATION METHOD(S):		COATS/LAYER:	FOOD SAFE? **YES NO**

GLAZE FIRING 1   DATE

KILN TYPE:	PROGRAM OR FIRING METHOD:	CONE:
PREHEAT/HOLD/COOL FIRING TIME/TEMP(S):		TOTAL TIME:

GLAZE/LUSTER FIRING   DATE

KILN TYPE:	PROGRAM OR FIRING METHOD:	CONE:
PREHEAT/HOLD/COOL FIRING TIME/TEMP(S):		TOTAL TIME:

NOTES:

____

____

____

____

SALES RECORD

SALE LOCATION:		ESTIMATED VALUE/LISTING PRICE:
SALE DATE:	TRANSACTION DETAILS:	FINAL PRICE:

PROJECT: **DATE:**

IMAGE or SKETCH

DIMENSIONS: **WEIGHT:**

CLAY

TYPE:		COLOR:	SOURCE:
ADDITIVE(S):			RESULTS RATING:

FORMING TECHNIQUE(S):

DECORATING TECHNIQUES & TOOLS:

DRYING TIME/NOTES:

BISQUE FIRING   DATE

KILN TYPE:	PROGRAM OR FIRING METHOD:	CONE:
PREHEAT/HOLD/COOL FIRING TIME/TEMP(S):		TOTAL TIME:
STAINS/SPRAYS/COMBUSTIBLES:		

Glaze(s)

BRAND:	COLOR/TRANSPARENCY/CHARACTERISTICS		
APPLICATION METHOD(S):		COATS/LAYER:	FOOD SAFE? **YES NO**

BRAND:	COLOR/TRANSPARENCY/CHARACTERISTICS		
APPLICATION METHOD(S):		COATS/LAYER:	FOOD SAFE? **YES NO**

BRAND:	COLOR/TRANSPARENCY/CHARACTERISTICS		
APPLICATION METHOD(S):		COATS/LAYER:	FOOD SAFE? **YES NO**

BRAND:	COLOR/TRANSPARENCY/CHARACTERISTICS		
APPLICATION METHOD(S):		COATS/LAYER:	FOOD SAFE? **YES NO**

BRAND:	COLOR/TRANSPARENCY/CHARACTERISTICS		
APPLICATION METHOD(S):		COATS/LAYER:	FOOD SAFE? **YES NO**

GLAZE FIRING 1   DATE

KILN TYPE:	PROGRAM OR FIRING METHOD:	CONE:
PREHEAT/HOLD/COOL FIRING TIME/TEMP(S):		TOTAL TIME:

GLAZE/LUSTER FIRING   DATE

KILN TYPE:	PROGRAM OR FIRING METHOD:	CONE:
PREHEAT/HOLD/COOL FIRING TIME/TEMP(S):		TOTAL TIME:

NOTES:

____

____

____

____

____

SALES RECORD

SALE LOCATION:		ESTIMATED VALUE/LISTING PRICE:	
SALE DATE:	TRANSACTION DETAILS:		FINAL PRICE:

PROJECT: **DATE:**

IMAGE or SKETCH

DIMENSIONS: WEIGHT:

CLAY

TYPE:		COLOR:	SOURCE:	
ADDITIVE(S):				RESULTS RATING:

FORMING TECHNIQUE(S):

____

____

DECORATING TECHNIQUES & TOOLS:

____

____

DRYING TIME/NOTES:

____

BISQUE FIRING   DATE

KILN TYPE:	PROGRAM OR FIRING METHOD:	CONE:
PREHEAT/HOLD/COOL FIRING TIME/TEMP(S):		TOTAL TIME:
STAINS/SPRAYS/COMBUSTIBLES:		

Glaze(s)

BRAND:	COLOR/TRANSPARENCY/CHARACTERISTICS		
APPLICATION METHOD(S):		COATS/LAYER:	FOOD SAFE? **YES NO**

BRAND:	COLOR/TRANSPARENCY/CHARACTERISTICS		
APPLICATION METHOD(S):		COATS/LAYER:	FOOD SAFE? **YES NO**

BRAND:	COLOR/TRANSPARENCY/CHARACTERISTICS		
APPLICATION METHOD(S):		COATS/LAYER:	FOOD SAFE? **YES NO**

BRAND:	COLOR/TRANSPARENCY/CHARACTERISTICS		
APPLICATION METHOD(S):		COATS/LAYER:	FOOD SAFE? **YES NO**

BRAND:	COLOR/TRANSPARENCY/CHARACTERISTICS		
APPLICATION METHOD(S):		COATS/LAYER:	FOOD SAFE? **YES NO**

GLAZE FIRING 1   DATE

KILN TYPE:	PROGRAM OR FIRING METHOD:	CONE:
PREHEAT/HOLD/COOL FIRING TIME/TEMP(S):		TOTAL TIME:

GLAZE/LUSTER FIRING   DATE

KILN TYPE:	PROGRAM OR FIRING METHOD:	CONE:
PREHEAT/HOLD/COOL FIRING TIME/TEMP(S):		TOTAL TIME:

NOTES:

____

____

____

____

SALES RECORD

SALE LOCATION:		ESTIMATED VALUE/LISTING PRICE:
SALE DATE:	TRANSACTION DETAILS:	FINAL PRICE:

PROJECT: **DATE:**

IMAGE or SKETCH

DIMENSIONS: WEIGHT:

CLAY

TYPE:	COLOR:	SOURCE:
ADDITIVE(S):		RESULTS RATING:

FORMING TECHNIQUE(S):

DECORATING TECHNIQUES & TOOLS:

DRYING TIME/NOTES:

BISQUE FIRING   DATE

KILN TYPE:	PROGRAM OR FIRING METHOD:	CONE:
PREHEAT/HOLD/COOL FIRING TIME/TEMP(S):		TOTAL TIME:
STAINS/SPRAYS/COMBUSTIBLES:		

Glaze(s)

BRAND:	COLOR/TRANSPARENCY/CHARACTERISTICS		
APPLICATION METHOD(S):		COATS/LAYER:	FOOD SAFE? **YES NO**

BRAND:	COLOR/TRANSPARENCY/CHARACTERISTICS		
APPLICATION METHOD(S):		COATS/LAYER:	FOOD SAFE? **YES NO**

BRAND:	COLOR/TRANSPARENCY/CHARACTERISTICS		
APPLICATION METHOD(S):		COATS/LAYER:	FOOD SAFE? **YES NO**

BRAND:	COLOR/TRANSPARENCY/CHARACTERISTICS		
APPLICATION METHOD(S):		COATS/LAYER:	FOOD SAFE? **YES NO**

BRAND:	COLOR/TRANSPARENCY/CHARACTERISTICS		
APPLICATION METHOD(S):		COATS/LAYER:	FOOD SAFE? **YES NO**

GLAZE FIRING 1   DATE

KILN TYPE:	PROGRAM OR FIRING METHOD:	CONE:
PREHEAT/HOLD/COOL FIRING TIME/TEMP(S):		TOTAL TIME:

GLAZE/LUSTER FIRING   DATE

KILN TYPE:	PROGRAM OR FIRING METHOD:	CONE:
PREHEAT/HOLD/COOL FIRING TIME/TEMP(S):		TOTAL TIME:

NOTES:

____

____

____

____

____

SALES RECORD

SALE LOCATION:	ESTIMATED VALUE/LISTING PRICE:
SALE DATE:	TRANSACTION DETAILS:	FINAL PRICE:

PROJECT: **DATE:**

IMAGE or SKETCH

DIMENSIONS: WEIGHT:

CLAY

TYPE:	COLOR:	SOURCE:
ADDITIVE(S):		RESULTS RATING:

FORMING TECHNIQUE(S):

DECORATING TECHNIQUES & TOOLS:

DRYING TIME/NOTES:

BISQUE FIRING   DATE

KILN TYPE:	PROGRAM OR FIRING METHOD:	CONE:
PREHEAT/HOLD/COOL FIRING TIME/TEMP(S):		TOTAL TIME:
STAINS/SPRAYS/COMBUSTIBLES:		

Glaze(s)

BRAND:	COLOR/TRANSPARENCY/CHARACTERISTICS		
APPLICATION METHOD(S):		COATS/LAYER:	FOOD SAFE? YES NO

BRAND:	COLOR/TRANSPARENCY/CHARACTERISTICS		
APPLICATION METHOD(S):		COATS/LAYER:	FOOD SAFE? YES NO

BRAND:	COLOR/TRANSPARENCY/CHARACTERISTICS		
APPLICATION METHOD(S):		COATS/LAYER:	FOOD SAFE? YES NO

BRAND:	COLOR/TRANSPARENCY/CHARACTERISTICS		
APPLICATION METHOD(S):		COATS/LAYER:	FOOD SAFE? YES NO

BRAND:	COLOR/TRANSPARENCY/CHARACTERISTICS		
APPLICATION METHOD(S):		COATS/LAYER:	FOOD SAFE? YES NO

GLAZE FIRING 1   DATE

KILN TYPE:	PROGRAM OR FIRING METHOD:	CONE:
PREHEAT/HOLD/COOL FIRING TIME/TEMP(S):		TOTAL TIME:

GLAZE/LUSTER FIRING   DATE

KILN TYPE:	PROGRAM OR FIRING METHOD:	CONE:
PREHEAT/HOLD/COOL FIRING TIME/TEMP(S):		TOTAL TIME:

NOTES:

____

____

____

____

____

SALES RECORD

SALE LOCATION:	ESTIMATED VALUE/LISTING PRICE:
SALE DATE: TRANSACTION DETAILS:	FINAL PRICE:

PROJECT: **DATE:**

IMAGE or SKETCH

DIMENSIONS: WEIGHT:

CLAY

TYPE:	COLOR:	SOURCE:

ADDITIVE(S):	RESULTS RATING:

FORMING TECHNIQUE(S):

DECORATING TECHNIQUES & TOOLS:

DRYING TIME/NOTES:

BISQUE FIRING   DATE

KILN TYPE:	PROGRAM OR FIRING METHOD:	CONE:

PREHEAT/HOLD/COOL FIRING TIME/TEMP(S):	TOTAL TIME:

STAINS/SPRAYS/COMBUSTIBLES:

Glaze(s)

BRAND:	COLOR/TRANSPARENCY/CHARACTERISTICS		
APPLICATION METHOD(S):		COATS/LAYER:	FOOD SAFE? **YES NO**

BRAND:	COLOR/TRANSPARENCY/CHARACTERISTICS		
APPLICATION METHOD(S):		COATS/LAYER:	FOOD SAFE? **YES NO**

BRAND:	COLOR/TRANSPARENCY/CHARACTERISTICS		
APPLICATION METHOD(S):		COATS/LAYER:	FOOD SAFE? **YES NO**

BRAND:	COLOR/TRANSPARENCY/CHARACTERISTICS		
APPLICATION METHOD(S):		COATS/LAYER:	FOOD SAFE? **YES NO**

BRAND:	COLOR/TRANSPARENCY/CHARACTERISTICS		
APPLICATION METHOD(S):		COATS/LAYER:	FOOD SAFE? **YES NO**

GLAZE FIRING 1   DATE

KILN TYPE:	PROGRAM OR FIRING METHOD:	CONE:
PREHEAT/HOLD/COOL FIRING TIME/TEMP(S):		TOTAL TIME:

GLAZE/LUSTER FIRING   DATE

KILN TYPE:	PROGRAM OR FIRING METHOD:	CONE:
PREHEAT/HOLD/COOL FIRING TIME/TEMP(S):		TOTAL TIME:

NOTES:

____

____

____

____

____

SALES RECORD

SALE LOCATION:	ESTIMATED VALUE/LISTING PRICE:
SALE DATE:	TRANSACTION DETAILS:	FINAL PRICE:

PROJECT: **DATE:**

IMAGE or SKETCH

DIMENSIONS: WEIGHT:

CLAY

TYPE:		COLOR:	SOURCE:	
ADDITIVE(S):				RESULTS RATING:

FORMING TECHNIQUE(S):

DECORATING TECHNIQUES & TOOLS:

DRYING TIME/NOTES:

BISQUE FIRING   DATE

KILN TYPE:	PROGRAM OR FIRING METHOD:	CONE:
PREHEAT/HOLD/COOL FIRING TIME/TEMP(S):		TOTAL TIME:
STAINS/SPRAYS/COMBUSTIBLES:		

Glaze(s)

BRAND:	COLOR/TRANSPARENCY/CHARACTERISTICS		
APPLICATION METHOD(S):		COATS/LAYER:	FOOD SAFE? **YES NO**

BRAND:	COLOR/TRANSPARENCY/CHARACTERISTICS		
APPLICATION METHOD(S):		COATS/LAYER:	FOOD SAFE? **YES NO**

BRAND:	COLOR/TRANSPARENCY/CHARACTERISTICS		
APPLICATION METHOD(S):		COATS/LAYER:	FOOD SAFE? **YES NO**

BRAND:	COLOR/TRANSPARENCY/CHARACTERISTICS		
APPLICATION METHOD(S):		COATS/LAYER:	FOOD SAFE? **YES NO**

BRAND:	COLOR/TRANSPARENCY/CHARACTERISTICS		
APPLICATION METHOD(S):		COATS/LAYER:	FOOD SAFE? **YES NO**

GLAZE FIRING 1   DATE

KILN TYPE:	PROGRAM OR FIRING METHOD:	CONE:
PREHEAT/HOLD/COOL FIRING TIME/TEMP(S):		TOTAL TIME:

GLAZE/LUSTER FIRING   DATE

KILN TYPE:	PROGRAM OR FIRING METHOD:	CONE:
PREHEAT/HOLD/COOL FIRING TIME/TEMP(S):		TOTAL TIME:

NOTES:

____

____

____

____

SALES RECORD

SALE LOCATION:	ESTIMATED VALUE/LISTING PRICE:
SALE DATE:	TRANSACTION DETAILS:	FINAL PRICE:

PROJECT: **DATE:**

IMAGE or SKETCH

DIMENSIONS: WEIGHT:

CLAY

TYPE:		COLOR:	SOURCE:
ADDITIVE(S):			RESULTS RATING:

FORMING TECHNIQUE(S):

DECORATING TECHNIQUES & TOOLS:

DRYING TIME/NOTES:

BISQUE FIRING   DATE

KILN TYPE:	PROGRAM OR FIRING METHOD:		CONE:
PREHEAT/HOLD/COOL FIRING TIME/TEMP(S):			TOTAL TIME:
STAINS/SPRAYS/COMBUSTIBLES:			

Glaze(s)

BRAND:	COLOR/TRANSPARENCY/CHARACTERISTICS		
APPLICATION METHOD(S):		COATS/LAYER:	FOOD SAFE? **YES NO**

BRAND:	COLOR/TRANSPARENCY/CHARACTERISTICS		
APPLICATION METHOD(S):		COATS/LAYER:	FOOD SAFE? **YES NO**

BRAND:	COLOR/TRANSPARENCY/CHARACTERISTICS		
APPLICATION METHOD(S):		COATS/LAYER:	FOOD SAFE? **YES NO**

BRAND:	COLOR/TRANSPARENCY/CHARACTERISTICS		
APPLICATION METHOD(S):		COATS/LAYER:	FOOD SAFE? **YES NO**

BRAND:	COLOR/TRANSPARENCY/CHARACTERISTICS		
APPLICATION METHOD(S):		COATS/LAYER:	FOOD SAFE? **YES NO**

GLAZE FIRING 1   DATE

KILN TYPE:	PROGRAM OR FIRING METHOD:	CONE:
PREHEAT/HOLD/COOL FIRING TIME/TEMP(S):		TOTAL TIME:

GLAZE/LUSTER FIRING   DATE

KILN TYPE:	PROGRAM OR FIRING METHOD:	CONE:
PREHEAT/HOLD/COOL FIRING TIME/TEMP(S):		TOTAL TIME:

NOTES:

____

____

____

____

____

SALES RECORD

SALE LOCATION:	ESTIMATED VALUE/LISTING PRICE:
SALE DATE:	TRANSACTION DETAILS:	FINAL PRICE:

PROJECT: _________________________________   **DATE:** _______________

DIMENSIONS: _________________________________   WEIGHT: _______________

CLAY

TYPE:	COLOR:	SOURCE:
ADDITIVE(S):		RESULTS RATING:

FORMING TECHNIQUE(S):
____
____

DECORATING TECHNIQUES & TOOLS:
____
____

DRYING TIME/NOTES:
____

BISQUE FIRING   DATE

KILN TYPE:	PROGRAM OR FIRING METHOD:	CONE:
PREHEAT/HOLD/COOL FIRING TIME/TEMP(S):		TOTAL TIME:
STAINS/SPRAYS/COMBUSTIBLES:		

Glaze(s)

BRAND:	COLOR/TRANSPARENCY/CHARACTERISTICS		
APPLICATION METHOD(S):		COATS/LAYER:	FOOD SAFE? YES NO

BRAND:	COLOR/TRANSPARENCY/CHARACTERISTICS		
APPLICATION METHOD(S):		COATS/LAYER:	FOOD SAFE? YES NO

BRAND:	COLOR/TRANSPARENCY/CHARACTERISTICS		
APPLICATION METHOD(S):		COATS/LAYER:	FOOD SAFE? YES NO

BRAND:	COLOR/TRANSPARENCY/CHARACTERISTICS		
APPLICATION METHOD(S):		COATS/LAYER:	FOOD SAFE? YES NO

BRAND:	COLOR/TRANSPARENCY/CHARACTERISTICS		
APPLICATION METHOD(S):		COATS/LAYER:	FOOD SAFE? YES NO

GLAZE FIRING 1   DATE

KILN TYPE:	PROGRAM OR FIRING METHOD:	CONE:
PREHEAT/HOLD/COOL FIRING TIME/TEMP(S):		TOTAL TIME:

GLAZE/LUSTER FIRING   DATE

KILN TYPE:	PROGRAM OR FIRING METHOD:	CONE:
PREHEAT/HOLD/COOL FIRING TIME/TEMP(S):		TOTAL TIME:

NOTES:

____

____

____

____

____

SALES RECORD

SALE LOCATION:	ESTIMATED VALUE/LISTING PRICE:
SALE DATE: TRANSACTION DETAILS:	FINAL PRICE:

PROJECT: **DATE:**

IMAGE or SKETCH

DIMENSIONS: **WEIGHT:**

CLAY

TYPE:	COLOR:	SOURCE:
ADDITIVE(S):		RESULTS RATING:

FORMING TECHNIQUE(S):

DECORATING TECHNIQUES & TOOLS:

DRYING TIME/NOTES:

BISQUE FIRING   DATE

KILN TYPE:	PROGRAM OR FIRING METHOD:	CONE:
PREHEAT/HOLD/COOL FIRING TIME/TEMP(S):		TOTAL TIME:
STAINS/SPRAYS/COMBUSTIBLES:		

Glaze(s)

BRAND:	COLOR/TRANSPARENCY/CHARACTERISTICS		
APPLICATION METHOD(S):		COATS/LAYER:	FOOD SAFE? **YES NO**

BRAND:	COLOR/TRANSPARENCY/CHARACTERISTICS		
APPLICATION METHOD(S):		COATS/LAYER:	FOOD SAFE? **YES NO**

BRAND:	COLOR/TRANSPARENCY/CHARACTERISTICS		
APPLICATION METHOD(S):		COATS/LAYER:	FOOD SAFE? **YES NO**

BRAND:	COLOR/TRANSPARENCY/CHARACTERISTICS		
APPLICATION METHOD(S):		COATS/LAYER:	FOOD SAFE? **YES NO**

BRAND:	COLOR/TRANSPARENCY/CHARACTERISTICS		
APPLICATION METHOD(S):		COATS/LAYER:	FOOD SAFE? **YES NO**

GLAZE FIRING 1   DATE

KILN TYPE:	PROGRAM OR FIRING METHOD:	CONE:
PREHEAT/HOLD/COOL FIRING TIME/TEMP(S):		TOTAL TIME:

GLAZE/LUSTER FIRING   DATE

KILN TYPE:	PROGRAM OR FIRING METHOD:	CONE:
PREHEAT/HOLD/COOL FIRING TIME/TEMP(S):		TOTAL TIME:

NOTES:

____

____

____

____

____

SALES RECORD

SALE LOCATION:	ESTIMATED VALUE/LISTING PRICE:
SALE DATE: TRANSACTION DETAILS:	FINAL PRICE:

PROJECT: **DATE:**

IMAGE or SKETCH

DIMENSIONS: WEIGHT:

CLAY

TYPE:	COLOR:	SOURCE:
ADDITIVE(S):		RESULTS RATING:

FORMING TECHNIQUE(S):

DECORATING TECHNIQUES & TOOLS:

DRYING TIME/NOTES:

BISQUE FIRING   DATE

KILN TYPE:	PROGRAM OR FIRING METHOD:	CONE:
PREHEAT/HOLD/COOL FIRING TIME/TEMP(S):		TOTAL TIME:
STAINS/SPRAYS/COMBUSTIBLES:		

Glaze(s)

BRAND:	COLOR/TRANSPARENCY/CHARACTERISTICS		
APPLICATION METHOD(S):		COATS/LAYER:	FOOD SAFE? YES NO

BRAND:	COLOR/TRANSPARENCY/CHARACTERISTICS		
APPLICATION METHOD(S):		COATS/LAYER:	FOOD SAFE? YES NO

BRAND:	COLOR/TRANSPARENCY/CHARACTERISTICS		
APPLICATION METHOD(S):		COATS/LAYER:	FOOD SAFE? YES NO

BRAND:	COLOR/TRANSPARENCY/CHARACTERISTICS		
APPLICATION METHOD(S):		COATS/LAYER:	FOOD SAFE? YES NO

BRAND:	COLOR/TRANSPARENCY/CHARACTERISTICS		
APPLICATION METHOD(S):		COATS/LAYER:	FOOD SAFE? YES NO

GLAZE FIRING 1   DATE

KILN TYPE:	PROGRAM OR FIRING METHOD:	CONE:
PREHEAT/HOLD/COOL FIRING TIME/TEMP(S):		TOTAL TIME:

GLAZE/LUSTER FIRING   DATE

KILN TYPE:	PROGRAM OR FIRING METHOD:	CONE:
PREHEAT/HOLD/COOL FIRING TIME/TEMP(S):		TOTAL TIME:

NOTES:
____

____

____

____

____

SALES RECORD

SALE LOCATION:	ESTIMATED VALUE/LISTING PRICE:	
SALE DATE:	TRANSACTION DETAILS:	FINAL PRICE:

PROJECT: **DATE:**

IMAGE or SKETCH

DIMENSIONS: **WEIGHT:**

CLAY

TYPE:	COLOR:	SOURCE:
ADDITIVE(S):		RESULTS RATING:

FORMING TECHNIQUE(S):

DECORATING TECHNIQUES & TOOLS:

DRYING TIME/NOTES:

BISQUE FIRING   DATE

KILN TYPE:	PROGRAM OR FIRING METHOD:	CONE:
PREHEAT/HOLD/COOL FIRING TIME/TEMP(S):		TOTAL TIME:
STAINS/SPRAYS/COMBUSTIBLES:		

Glaze(s)

BRAND:	COLOR/TRANSPARENCY/CHARACTERISTICS		
APPLICATION METHOD(S):		COATS/LAYER:	FOOD SAFE? **YES NO**

BRAND:	COLOR/TRANSPARENCY/CHARACTERISTICS		
APPLICATION METHOD(S):		COATS/LAYER:	FOOD SAFE? **YES NO**

BRAND:	COLOR/TRANSPARENCY/CHARACTERISTICS		
APPLICATION METHOD(S):		COATS/LAYER:	FOOD SAFE? **YES NO**

BRAND:	COLOR/TRANSPARENCY/CHARACTERISTICS		
APPLICATION METHOD(S):		COATS/LAYER:	FOOD SAFE? **YES NO**

BRAND:	COLOR/TRANSPARENCY/CHARACTERISTICS		
APPLICATION METHOD(S):		COATS/LAYER:	FOOD SAFE? **YES NO**

GLAZE FIRING 1   DATE

KILN TYPE:	PROGRAM OR FIRING METHOD:	CONE:
PREHEAT/HOLD/COOL FIRING TIME/TEMP(S):		TOTAL TIME:

GLAZE/LUSTER FIRING   DATE

KILN TYPE:	PROGRAM OR FIRING METHOD:	CONE:
PREHEAT/HOLD/COOL FIRING TIME/TEMP(S):		TOTAL TIME:

NOTES:

____

____

____

____

____

SALES RECORD

SALE LOCATION:	ESTIMATED VALUE/LISTING PRICE:

SALE DATE:	TRANSACTION DETAILS:	FINAL PRICE:

PROJECT: **DATE:**

IMAGE or SKETCH

DIMENSIONS: **WEIGHT:**

CLAY

TYPE:	COLOR:	SOURCE:
ADDITIVE(S):		RESULTS RATING:

FORMING TECHNIQUE(S):

DECORATING TECHNIQUES & TOOLS:

DRYING TIME/NOTES:

BISQUE FIRING   DATE

KILN TYPE:	PROGRAM OR FIRING METHOD:	CONE:
PREHEAT/HOLD/COOL FIRING TIME/TEMP(S):		TOTAL TIME:
STAINS/SPRAYS/COMBUSTIBLES:		

Glaze(s)

BRAND:	COLOR/TRANSPARENCY/CHARACTERISTICS		
APPLICATION METHOD(S):		COATS/LAYER:	FOOD SAFE? **YES NO**

BRAND:	COLOR/TRANSPARENCY/CHARACTERISTICS		
APPLICATION METHOD(S):		COATS/LAYER:	FOOD SAFE? **YES NO**

BRAND:	COLOR/TRANSPARENCY/CHARACTERISTICS		
APPLICATION METHOD(S):		COATS/LAYER:	FOOD SAFE? **YES NO**

BRAND:	COLOR/TRANSPARENCY/CHARACTERISTICS		
APPLICATION METHOD(S):		COATS/LAYER:	FOOD SAFE? **YES NO**

BRAND:	COLOR/TRANSPARENCY/CHARACTERISTICS		
APPLICATION METHOD(S):		COATS/LAYER:	FOOD SAFE? **YES NO**

GLAZE FIRING 1   DATE

KILN TYPE:	PROGRAM OR FIRING METHOD:	CONE:
PREHEAT/HOLD/COOL FIRING TIME/TEMP(S):		TOTAL TIME:

GLAZE/LUSTER FIRING   DATE

KILN TYPE:	PROGRAM OR FIRING METHOD:	CONE:
PREHEAT/HOLD/COOL FIRING TIME/TEMP(S):		TOTAL TIME:

NOTES:

____

____

____

____

____

SALES RECORD

SALE LOCATION:	ESTIMATED VALUE/LISTING PRICE:
SALE DATE:	TRANSACTION DETAILS:	FINAL PRICE:

PROJECT: **DATE:**

IMAGE or SKETCH

DIMENSIONS: WEIGHT:

CLAY

TYPE:	COLOR:	SOURCE:
ADDITIVE(S):		RESULTS RATING:

FORMING TECHNIQUE(S):

DECORATING TECHNIQUES & TOOLS:

DRYING TIME/NOTES:

BISQUE FIRING   DATE

KILN TYPE:	PROGRAM OR FIRING METHOD:	CONE:
PREHEAT/HOLD/COOL FIRING TIME/TEMP(S):		TOTAL TIME:
STAINS/SPRAYS/COMBUSTIBLES:		

Glaze(s)

BRAND:	COLOR/TRANSPARENCY/CHARACTERISTICS		
APPLICATION METHOD(S):		COATS/LAYER:	FOOD SAFE? **YES NO**

BRAND:	COLOR/TRANSPARENCY/CHARACTERISTICS		
APPLICATION METHOD(S):		COATS/LAYER:	FOOD SAFE? **YES NO**

BRAND:	COLOR/TRANSPARENCY/CHARACTERISTICS		
APPLICATION METHOD(S):		COATS/LAYER:	FOOD SAFE? **YES NO**

BRAND:	COLOR/TRANSPARENCY/CHARACTERISTICS		
APPLICATION METHOD(S):		COATS/LAYER:	FOOD SAFE? **YES NO**

BRAND:	COLOR/TRANSPARENCY/CHARACTERISTICS		
APPLICATION METHOD(S):		COATS/LAYER:	FOOD SAFE? **YES NO**

GLAZE FIRING 1   DATE

KILN TYPE:	PROGRAM OR FIRING METHOD:	CONE:
PREHEAT/HOLD/COOL FIRING TIME/TEMP(S):		TOTAL TIME:

GLAZE/LUSTER FIRING   DATE

KILN TYPE:	PROGRAM OR FIRING METHOD:	CONE:
PREHEAT/HOLD/COOL FIRING TIME/TEMP(S):		TOTAL TIME:

NOTES:

____

____

____

____

SALES RECORD

SALE LOCATION:	ESTIMATED VALUE/LISTING PRICE:
SALE DATE:	TRANSACTION DETAILS:	FINAL PRICE:

PROJECT: **DATE:**

IMAGE or SKETCH

DIMENSIONS: WEIGHT:

CLAY

TYPE:		COLOR:	SOURCE:	
ADDITIVE(S):				RESULTS RATING:

FORMING TECHNIQUE(S):

____

____

DECORATING TECHNIQUES & TOOLS:

____

____

DRYING TIME/NOTES:

____

BISQUE FIRING   DATE

KILN TYPE:	PROGRAM OR FIRING METHOD:	CONE:
PREHEAT/HOLD/COOL FIRING TIME/TEMP(S):		TOTAL TIME:
STAINS/SPRAYS/COMBUSTIBLES:		

Glaze(s)

BRAND:	COLOR/TRANSPARENCY/CHARACTERISTICS		
APPLICATION METHOD(S):		COATS/LAYER:	FOOD SAFE? **YES NO**

BRAND:	COLOR/TRANSPARENCY/CHARACTERISTICS		
APPLICATION METHOD(S):		COATS/LAYER:	FOOD SAFE? **YES NO**

BRAND:	COLOR/TRANSPARENCY/CHARACTERISTICS		
APPLICATION METHOD(S):		COATS/LAYER:	FOOD SAFE? **YES NO**

BRAND:	COLOR/TRANSPARENCY/CHARACTERISTICS		
APPLICATION METHOD(S):		COATS/LAYER:	FOOD SAFE? **YES NO**

BRAND:	COLOR/TRANSPARENCY/CHARACTERISTICS		
APPLICATION METHOD(S):		COATS/LAYER:	FOOD SAFE? **YES NO**

GLAZE FIRING 1   DATE

KILN TYPE:	PROGRAM OR FIRING METHOD:	CONE:
PREHEAT/HOLD/COOL FIRING TIME/TEMP(S):		TOTAL TIME:

GLAZE/LUSTER FIRING   DATE

KILN TYPE:	PROGRAM OR FIRING METHOD:	CONE:
PREHEAT/HOLD/COOL FIRING TIME/TEMP(S):		TOTAL TIME:

NOTES:

____

____

____

____

____

SALES RECORD

SALE LOCATION:		ESTIMATED VALUE/LISTING PRICE:
SALE DATE:	TRANSACTION DETAILS:	FINAL PRICE:

PROJECT: **DATE:**

IMAGE or SKETCH

DIMENSIONS: WEIGHT:

CLAY

TYPE:		COLOR:	SOURCE:	
ADDITIVE(S):				RESULTS RATING:

FORMING TECHNIQUE(S):

____

____

DECORATING TECHNIQUES & TOOLS:

____

____

DRYING TIME/NOTES:

____

____

BISQUE FIRING   DATE

KILN TYPE:	PROGRAM OR FIRING METHOD:	CONE:
PREHEAT/HOLD/COOL FIRING TIME/TEMP(S):		TOTAL TIME:
STAINS/SPRAYS/COMBUSTIBLES:		

Glaze(s)

BRAND:	COLOR/TRANSPARENCY/CHARACTERISTICS		
APPLICATION METHOD(S):		COATS/LAYER:	FOOD SAFE? **YES NO**

BRAND:	COLOR/TRANSPARENCY/CHARACTERISTICS		
APPLICATION METHOD(S):		COATS/LAYER:	FOOD SAFE? **YES NO**

BRAND:	COLOR/TRANSPARENCY/CHARACTERISTICS		
APPLICATION METHOD(S):		COATS/LAYER:	FOOD SAFE? **YES NO**

BRAND:	COLOR/TRANSPARENCY/CHARACTERISTICS		
APPLICATION METHOD(S):		COATS/LAYER:	FOOD SAFE? **YES NO**

BRAND:	COLOR/TRANSPARENCY/CHARACTERISTICS		
APPLICATION METHOD(S):		COATS/LAYER:	FOOD SAFE? **YES NO**

GLAZE FIRING 1   DATE

KILN TYPE:	PROGRAM OR FIRING METHOD:	CONE:
PREHEAT/HOLD/COOL FIRING TIME/TEMP(S):		TOTAL TIME:

GLAZE/LUSTER FIRING   DATE

KILN TYPE:	PROGRAM OR FIRING METHOD:	CONE:
PREHEAT/HOLD/COOL FIRING TIME/TEMP(S):		TOTAL TIME:

NOTES:

____

____

____

____

SALES RECORD

SALE LOCATION:	ESTIMATED VALUE/LISTING PRICE:
SALE DATE:	TRANSACTION DETAILS:	FINAL PRICE:

PROJECT: **DATE:**

IMAGE or SKETCH

DIMENSIONS: WEIGHT:

CLAY

TYPE:	COLOR:	SOURCE:
ADDITIVE(S):		RESULTS RATING:

FORMING TECHNIQUE(S):

DECORATING TECHNIQUES & TOOLS:

DRYING TIME/NOTES:

BISQUE FIRING   DATE

KILN TYPE:	PROGRAM OR FIRING METHOD:	CONE:
PREHEAT/HOLD/COOL FIRING TIME/TEMP(S):		TOTAL TIME:
STAINS/SPRAYS/COMBUSTIBLES:		

Glaze(s)

BRAND:	COLOR/TRANSPARENCY/CHARACTERISTICS		
APPLICATION METHOD(S):		COATS/LAYER:	FOOD SAFE? **YES NO**

BRAND:	COLOR/TRANSPARENCY/CHARACTERISTICS		
APPLICATION METHOD(S):		COATS/LAYER:	FOOD SAFE? **YES NO**

BRAND:	COLOR/TRANSPARENCY/CHARACTERISTICS		
APPLICATION METHOD(S):		COATS/LAYER:	FOOD SAFE? **YES NO**

BRAND:	COLOR/TRANSPARENCY/CHARACTERISTICS		
APPLICATION METHOD(S):		COATS/LAYER:	FOOD SAFE? **YES NO**

BRAND:	COLOR/TRANSPARENCY/CHARACTERISTICS		
APPLICATION METHOD(S):		COATS/LAYER:	FOOD SAFE? **YES NO**

GLAZE FIRING 1   DATE

KILN TYPE:	PROGRAM OR FIRING METHOD:	CONE:
PREHEAT/HOLD/COOL FIRING TIME/TEMP(S):		TOTAL TIME:

GLAZE/LUSTER FIRING   DATE

KILN TYPE:	PROGRAM OR FIRING METHOD:	CONE:
PREHEAT/HOLD/COOL FIRING TIME/TEMP(S):		TOTAL TIME:

NOTES:

____

____

____

____

____

SALES RECORD

SALE LOCATION:	ESTIMATED VALUE/LISTING PRICE:	
SALE DATE:	TRANSACTION DETAILS:	FINAL PRICE:

PROJECT: **DATE:**

IMAGE or SKETCH

DIMENSIONS: **WEIGHT:**

CLAY

TYPE:		COLOR:	SOURCE:	
ADDITIVE(S):				RESULTS RATING:

FORMING TECHNIQUE(S):

DECORATING TECHNIQUES & TOOLS:

DRYING TIME/NOTES:

BISQUE FIRING   DATE

KILN TYPE:	PROGRAM OR FIRING METHOD:	CONE:
PREHEAT/HOLD/COOL FIRING TIME/TEMP(S):		TOTAL TIME:
STAINS/SPRAYS/COMBUSTIBLES:		

Glaze(s)

BRAND:	COLOR/TRANSPARENCY/CHARACTERISTICS		
APPLICATION METHOD(S):		COATS/LAYER:	FOOD SAFE? **YES NO**

BRAND:	COLOR/TRANSPARENCY/CHARACTERISTICS		
APPLICATION METHOD(S):		COATS/LAYER:	FOOD SAFE? **YES NO**

BRAND:	COLOR/TRANSPARENCY/CHARACTERISTICS		
APPLICATION METHOD(S):		COATS/LAYER:	FOOD SAFE? **YES NO**

BRAND:	COLOR/TRANSPARENCY/CHARACTERISTICS		
APPLICATION METHOD(S):		COATS/LAYER:	FOOD SAFE? **YES NO**

BRAND:	COLOR/TRANSPARENCY/CHARACTERISTICS		
APPLICATION METHOD(S):		COATS/LAYER:	FOOD SAFE? **YES NO**

GLAZE FIRING 1   DATE

KILN TYPE:	PROGRAM OR FIRING METHOD:	CONE:
PREHEAT/HOLD/COOL FIRING TIME/TEMP(S):		TOTAL TIME:

GLAZE/LUSTER FIRING   DATE

KILN TYPE:	PROGRAM OR FIRING METHOD:	CONE:
PREHEAT/HOLD/COOL FIRING TIME/TEMP(S):		TOTAL TIME:

NOTES:

____

____

____

____

____

SALES RECORD

SALE LOCATION:	ESTIMATED VALUE/LISTING PRICE:	
SALE DATE:	TRANSACTION DETAILS:	FINAL PRICE:

PROJECT: **DATE:**

DIMENSIONS: WEIGHT:

CLAY

TYPE:	COLOR:	SOURCE:
ADDITIVE(S):		RESULTS RATING:

FORMING TECHNIQUE(S):

DECORATING TECHNIQUES & TOOLS:

DRYING TIME/NOTES:

BISQUE FIRING   DATE

KILN TYPE:	PROGRAM OR FIRING METHOD:	CONE:
PREHEAT/HOLD/COOL FIRING TIME/TEMP(S):		TOTAL TIME:
STAINS/SPRAYS/COMBUSTIBLES:		

Glaze(s)

BRAND:	COLOR/TRANSPARENCY/CHARACTERISTICS		
APPLICATION METHOD(S):		COATS/LAYER:	FOOD SAFE? **YES NO**

BRAND:	COLOR/TRANSPARENCY/CHARACTERISTICS		
APPLICATION METHOD(S):		COATS/LAYER:	FOOD SAFE? **YES NO**

BRAND:	COLOR/TRANSPARENCY/CHARACTERISTICS		
APPLICATION METHOD(S):		COATS/LAYER:	FOOD SAFE? **YES NO**

BRAND:	COLOR/TRANSPARENCY/CHARACTERISTICS		
APPLICATION METHOD(S):		COATS/LAYER:	FOOD SAFE? **YES NO**

BRAND:	COLOR/TRANSPARENCY/CHARACTERISTICS		
APPLICATION METHOD(S):		COATS/LAYER:	FOOD SAFE? **YES NO**

GLAZE FIRING 1   DATE

KILN TYPE:	PROGRAM OR FIRING METHOD:	CONE:
PREHEAT/HOLD/COOL FIRING TIME/TEMP(S):		TOTAL TIME:

GLAZE/LUSTER FIRING   DATE

KILN TYPE:	PROGRAM OR FIRING METHOD:	CONE:
PREHEAT/HOLD/COOL FIRING TIME/TEMP(S):		TOTAL TIME:

NOTES:

____

____

____

____

SALES RECORD

SALE LOCATION:	ESTIMATED VALUE/LISTING PRICE:
SALE DATE: TRANSACTION DETAILS:	FINAL PRICE:

PROJECT: DATE:

IMAGE or SKETCH

DIMENSIONS: WEIGHT:

CLAY

TYPE:	COLOR:	SOURCE:
ADDITIVE(S):		RESULTS RATING:

FORMING TECHNIQUE(S):

DECORATING TECHNIQUES & TOOLS:

DRYING TIME/NOTES:

BISQUE FIRING   DATE

KILN TYPE:	PROGRAM OR FIRING METHOD:	CONE:
PREHEAT/HOLD/COOL FIRING TIME/TEMP(S):		TOTAL TIME:
STAINS/SPRAYS/COMBUSTIBLES:		

Glaze(s)

BRAND:	COLOR/TRANSPARENCY/CHARACTERISTICS		
APPLICATION METHOD(S):		COATS/LAYER:	FOOD SAFE? **YES NO**

BRAND:	COLOR/TRANSPARENCY/CHARACTERISTICS		
APPLICATION METHOD(S):		COATS/LAYER:	FOOD SAFE? **YES NO**

BRAND:	COLOR/TRANSPARENCY/CHARACTERISTICS		
APPLICATION METHOD(S):		COATS/LAYER:	FOOD SAFE? **YES NO**

BRAND:	COLOR/TRANSPARENCY/CHARACTERISTICS		
APPLICATION METHOD(S):		COATS/LAYER:	FOOD SAFE? **YES NO**

BRAND:	COLOR/TRANSPARENCY/CHARACTERISTICS		
APPLICATION METHOD(S):		COATS/LAYER:	FOOD SAFE? **YES NO**

GLAZE FIRING 1   DATE

KILN TYPE:	PROGRAM OR FIRING METHOD:	CONE:
PREHEAT/HOLD/COOL FIRING TIME/TEMP(S):		TOTAL TIME:

GLAZE/LUSTER FIRING   DATE

KILN TYPE:	PROGRAM OR FIRING METHOD:	CONE:
PREHEAT/HOLD/COOL FIRING TIME/TEMP(S):		TOTAL TIME:

NOTES:

____

____

____

____

____

SALES RECORD

SALE LOCATION:	ESTIMATED VALUE/LISTING PRICE:
SALE DATE: TRANSACTION DETAILS:	FINAL PRICE:

PROJECT: **DATE:**

DIMENSIONS: WEIGHT:

CLAY

TYPE:		COLOR:	SOURCE:	
ADDITIVE(S):				RESULTS RATING:

FORMING TECHNIQUE(S):

DECORATING TECHNIQUES & TOOLS:

DRYING TIME/NOTES:

BISQUE FIRING   DATE

KILN TYPE:	PROGRAM OR FIRING METHOD:	CONE:
PREHEAT/HOLD/COOL FIRING TIME/TEMP(S):		TOTAL TIME:
STAINS/SPRAYS/COMBUSTIBLES:		

Glaze(s)

BRAND:	COLOR/TRANSPARENCY/CHARACTERISTICS		
APPLICATION METHOD(S):		COATS/LAYER:	FOOD SAFE? **YES NO**

BRAND:	COLOR/TRANSPARENCY/CHARACTERISTICS		
APPLICATION METHOD(S):		COATS/LAYER:	FOOD SAFE? **YES NO**

BRAND:	COLOR/TRANSPARENCY/CHARACTERISTICS		
APPLICATION METHOD(S):		COATS/LAYER:	FOOD SAFE? **YES NO**

BRAND:	COLOR/TRANSPARENCY/CHARACTERISTICS		
APPLICATION METHOD(S):		COATS/LAYER:	FOOD SAFE? **YES NO**

BRAND:	COLOR/TRANSPARENCY/CHARACTERISTICS		
APPLICATION METHOD(S):		COATS/LAYER:	FOOD SAFE? **YES NO**

GLAZE FIRING 1   DATE

KILN TYPE:	PROGRAM OR FIRING METHOD:	CONE:
PREHEAT/HOLD/COOL FIRING TIME/TEMP(S):		TOTAL TIME:

GLAZE/LUSTER FIRING   DATE

KILN TYPE:	PROGRAM OR FIRING METHOD:	CONE:
PREHEAT/HOLD/COOL FIRING TIME/TEMP(S):		TOTAL TIME:

NOTES:

____

____

____

____

____

SALES RECORD

SALE LOCATION:	ESTIMATED VALUE/LISTING PRICE:
SALE DATE:	TRANSACTION DETAILS:	FINAL PRICE:

PROJECT: **DATE:**

IMAGE or SKETCH

DIMENSIONS: WEIGHT:

CLAY

TYPE:		COLOR:	SOURCE:	
ADDITIVE(S):				RESULTS RATING:

FORMING TECHNIQUE(S):

DECORATING TECHNIQUES & TOOLS:

DRYING TIME/NOTES:

BISQUE FIRING   DATE

KILN TYPE:	PROGRAM OR FIRING METHOD:	CONE:
PREHEAT/HOLD/COOL FIRING TIME/TEMP(S):		TOTAL TIME:
STAINS/SPRAYS/COMBUSTIBLES:		

Glaze(s)

<table>
<tr><td>BRAND:</td><td colspan="2">COLOR/TRANSPARENCY/CHARACTERISTICS</td></tr>
<tr><td>APPLICATION METHOD(S):</td><td>COATS/LAYER:</td><td>FOOD SAFE?
YES   NO</td></tr>
</table>

<table>
<tr><td>BRAND:</td><td colspan="2">COLOR/TRANSPARENCY/CHARACTERISTICS</td></tr>
<tr><td>APPLICATION METHOD(S):</td><td>COATS/LAYER:</td><td>FOOD SAFE?
YES   NO</td></tr>
</table>

<table>
<tr><td>BRAND:</td><td colspan="2">COLOR/TRANSPARENCY/CHARACTERISTICS</td></tr>
<tr><td>APPLICATION METHOD(S):</td><td>COATS/LAYER:</td><td>FOOD SAFE?
YES   NO</td></tr>
</table>

<table>
<tr><td>BRAND:</td><td colspan="2">COLOR/TRANSPARENCY/CHARACTERISTICS</td></tr>
<tr><td>APPLICATION METHOD(S):</td><td>COATS/LAYER:</td><td>FOOD SAFE?
YES   NO</td></tr>
</table>

<table>
<tr><td>BRAND:</td><td colspan="2">COLOR/TRANSPARENCY/CHARACTERISTICS</td></tr>
<tr><td>APPLICATION METHOD(S):</td><td>COATS/LAYER:</td><td>FOOD SAFE?
YES   NO</td></tr>
</table>

GLAZE FIRING 1   DATE

<table>
<tr><td>KILN TYPE:</td><td>PROGRAM OR FIRING METHOD:</td><td>CONE:</td></tr>
<tr><td>PREHEAT/HOLD/COOL FIRING TIME/TEMP(S):</td><td></td><td>TOTAL TIME:</td></tr>
</table>

GLAZE/LUSTER FIRING   DATE

<table>
<tr><td>KILN TYPE:</td><td>PROGRAM OR FIRING METHOD:</td><td>CONE:</td></tr>
<tr><td>PREHEAT/HOLD/COOL FIRING TIME/TEMP(S):</td><td></td><td>TOTAL TIME:</td></tr>
</table>

NOTES:

____

____

____

____

____

SALES RECORD

<table>
<tr><td colspan="2">SALE LOCATION:</td><td>ESTIMATED VALUE/LISTING PRICE:</td></tr>
<tr><td>SALE DATE:</td><td>TRANSACTION DETAILS:</td><td>FINAL PRICE:</td></tr>
</table>

PROJECT: **DATE:**

IMAGE or SKETCH

DIMENSIONS: WEIGHT:

CLAY

TYPE:	COLOR:	SOURCE:
ADDITIVE(S):		RESULTS RATING:

FORMING TECHNIQUE(S):

DECORATING TECHNIQUES & TOOLS:

DRYING TIME/NOTES:

BISQUE FIRING   DATE

KILN TYPE:	PROGRAM OR FIRING METHOD:	CONE:
PREHEAT/HOLD/COOL FIRING TIME/TEMP(S):		TOTAL TIME:
STAINS/SPRAYS/COMBUSTIBLES:		

Glaze(s)

BRAND:	COLOR/TRANSPARENCY/CHARACTERISTICS		
APPLICATION METHOD(S):		COATS/LAYER:	FOOD SAFE? **YES NO**

BRAND:	COLOR/TRANSPARENCY/CHARACTERISTICS		
APPLICATION METHOD(S):		COATS/LAYER:	FOOD SAFE? **YES NO**

BRAND:	COLOR/TRANSPARENCY/CHARACTERISTICS		
APPLICATION METHOD(S):		COATS/LAYER:	FOOD SAFE? **YES NO**

BRAND:	COLOR/TRANSPARENCY/CHARACTERISTICS		
APPLICATION METHOD(S):		COATS/LAYER:	FOOD SAFE? **YES NO**

BRAND:	COLOR/TRANSPARENCY/CHARACTERISTICS		
APPLICATION METHOD(S):		COATS/LAYER:	FOOD SAFE? **YES NO**

GLAZE FIRING 1   DATE

KILN TYPE:	PROGRAM OR FIRING METHOD:	CONE:
PREHEAT/HOLD/COOL FIRING TIME/TEMP(S):		TOTAL TIME:

GLAZE/LUSTER FIRING   DATE

KILN TYPE:	PROGRAM OR FIRING METHOD:	CONE:
PREHEAT/HOLD/COOL FIRING TIME/TEMP(S):		TOTAL TIME:

NOTES:

____

____

____

____

____

SALES RECORD

SALE LOCATION:	ESTIMATED VALUE/LISTING PRICE:
SALE DATE: TRANSACTION DETAILS:	FINAL PRICE:

PROJECT:

DATE:

IMAGE or SKETCH

DIMENSIONS:

WEIGHT:

CLAY

TYPE:	COLOR:	SOURCE:
ADDITIVE(S):		RESULTS RATING:

FORMING TECHNIQUE(S):

DECORATING TECHNIQUES & TOOLS:

DRYING TIME/NOTES:

BISQUE FIRING   DATE

KILN TYPE:	PROGRAM OR FIRING METHOD:	CONE:
PREHEAT/HOLD/COOL FIRING TIME/TEMP(S):		TOTAL TIME:
STAINS/SPRAYS/COMBUSTIBLES:		

Glaze(s)

BRAND:	COLOR/TRANSPARENCY/CHARACTERISTICS		
APPLICATION METHOD(S):		COATS/LAYER:	FOOD SAFE? **YES NO**

BRAND:	COLOR/TRANSPARENCY/CHARACTERISTICS		
APPLICATION METHOD(S):		COATS/LAYER:	FOOD SAFE? **YES NO**

BRAND:	COLOR/TRANSPARENCY/CHARACTERISTICS		
APPLICATION METHOD(S):		COATS/LAYER:	FOOD SAFE? **YES NO**

BRAND:	COLOR/TRANSPARENCY/CHARACTERISTICS		
APPLICATION METHOD(S):		COATS/LAYER:	FOOD SAFE? **YES NO**

BRAND:	COLOR/TRANSPARENCY/CHARACTERISTICS		
APPLICATION METHOD(S):		COATS/LAYER:	FOOD SAFE? **YES NO**

GLAZE FIRING 1   DATE

KILN TYPE:	PROGRAM OR FIRING METHOD:	CONE:
PREHEAT/HOLD/COOL FIRING TIME/TEMP(S):		TOTAL TIME:

GLAZE/LUSTER FIRING   DATE

KILN TYPE:	PROGRAM OR FIRING METHOD:	CONE:
PREHEAT/HOLD/COOL FIRING TIME/TEMP(S):		TOTAL TIME:

NOTES:

____

____

____

____

____

SALES RECORD

SALE LOCATION:	ESTIMATED VALUE/LISTING PRICE:
SALE DATE:	TRANSACTION DETAILS:	FINAL PRICE:

PROJECT: **DATE:**

IMAGE or SKETCH

DIMENSIONS: **WEIGHT:**

CLAY

TYPE:	COLOR:	SOURCE:
ADDITIVE(S):		RESULTS RATING:

FORMING TECHNIQUE(S):

DECORATING TECHNIQUES & TOOLS:

DRYING TIME/NOTES:

BISQUE FIRING   DATE

KILN TYPE:	PROGRAM OR FIRING METHOD:	CONE:
PREHEAT/HOLD/COOL FIRING TIME/TEMP(S):		TOTAL TIME:
STAINS/SPRAYS/COMBUSTIBLES:		

Glaze(s)

BRAND:	COLOR/TRANSPARENCY/CHARACTERISTICS		
APPLICATION METHOD(S):		COATS/LAYER:	FOOD SAFE? **YES NO**

BRAND:	COLOR/TRANSPARENCY/CHARACTERISTICS		
APPLICATION METHOD(S):		COATS/LAYER:	FOOD SAFE? **YES NO**

BRAND:	COLOR/TRANSPARENCY/CHARACTERISTICS		
APPLICATION METHOD(S):		COATS/LAYER:	FOOD SAFE? **YES NO**

BRAND:	COLOR/TRANSPARENCY/CHARACTERISTICS		
APPLICATION METHOD(S):		COATS/LAYER:	FOOD SAFE? **YES NO**

BRAND:	COLOR/TRANSPARENCY/CHARACTERISTICS		
APPLICATION METHOD(S):		COATS/LAYER:	FOOD SAFE? **YES NO**

GLAZE FIRING 1   DATE

KILN TYPE:	PROGRAM OR FIRING METHOD:	CONE:
PREHEAT/HOLD/COOL FIRING TIME/TEMP(S):		TOTAL TIME:

GLAZE/LUSTER FIRING   DATE

KILN TYPE:	PROGRAM OR FIRING METHOD:	CONE:
PREHEAT/HOLD/COOL FIRING TIME/TEMP(S):		TOTAL TIME:

NOTES:

____

____

____

____

____

SALES RECORD

SALE LOCATION:	ESTIMATED VALUE/LISTING PRICE:
SALE DATE: TRANSACTION DETAILS:	FINAL PRICE:

PROJECT: **DATE:**

IMAGE or SKETCH

DIMENSIONS: WEIGHT:

CLAY

TYPE:	COLOR:	SOURCE:
ADDITIVE(S):		RESULTS RATING:

FORMING TECHNIQUE(S):

DECORATING TECHNIQUES & TOOLS:

DRYING TIME/NOTES:

BISQUE FIRING   DATE

KILN TYPE:	PROGRAM OR FIRING METHOD:	CONE:
PREHEAT/HOLD/COOL FIRING TIME/TEMP(S):		TOTAL TIME:
STAINS/SPRAYS/COMBUSTIBLES:		

Glaze(s)

<table>
<tr><td>BRAND:</td><td colspan="3">COLOR/TRANSPARENCY/CHARACTERISTICS</td></tr>
<tr><td>APPLICATION METHOD(S):</td><td>COATS/LAYER:</td><td colspan="2">FOOD SAFE?
YES NO</td></tr>
</table>

<table>
<tr><td>BRAND:</td><td colspan="3">COLOR/TRANSPARENCY/CHARACTERISTICS</td></tr>
<tr><td>APPLICATION METHOD(S):</td><td>COATS/LAYER:</td><td colspan="2">FOOD SAFE?
YES NO</td></tr>
</table>

<table>
<tr><td>BRAND:</td><td colspan="3">COLOR/TRANSPARENCY/CHARACTERISTICS</td></tr>
<tr><td>APPLICATION METHOD(S):</td><td>COATS/LAYER:</td><td colspan="2">FOOD SAFE?
YES NO</td></tr>
</table>

<table>
<tr><td>BRAND:</td><td colspan="3">COLOR/TRANSPARENCY/CHARACTERISTICS</td></tr>
<tr><td>APPLICATION METHOD(S):</td><td>COATS/LAYER:</td><td colspan="2">FOOD SAFE?
YES NO</td></tr>
</table>

<table>
<tr><td>BRAND:</td><td colspan="3">COLOR/TRANSPARENCY/CHARACTERISTICS</td></tr>
<tr><td>APPLICATION METHOD(S):</td><td>COATS/LAYER:</td><td colspan="2">FOOD SAFE?
YES NO</td></tr>
</table>

GLAZE FIRING 1   DATE

<table>
<tr><td>KILN TYPE:</td><td>PROGRAM OR FIRING METHOD:</td><td>CONE:</td></tr>
<tr><td>PREHEAT/HOLD/COOL FIRING TIME/TEMP(S):</td><td></td><td>TOTAL TIME:</td></tr>
</table>

GLAZE/LUSTER FIRING   DATE

<table>
<tr><td>KILN TYPE:</td><td>PROGRAM OR FIRING METHOD:</td><td>CONE:</td></tr>
<tr><td>PREHEAT/HOLD/COOL FIRING TIME/TEMP(S):</td><td></td><td>TOTAL TIME:</td></tr>
</table>

NOTES:

____

____

____

____

____

SALES RECORD

<table>
<tr><td>SALE LOCATION:</td><td>ESTIMATED VALUE/LISTING PRICE:</td></tr>
<tr><td>SALE DATE:</td><td>TRANSACTION DETAILS:</td><td>FINAL PRICE:</td></tr>
</table>

PROJECT: **DATE:**

IMAGE or SKETCH

DIMENSIONS: **WEIGHT:**

CLAY

TYPE:	COLOR:	SOURCE:
ADDITIVE(S):		RESULTS RATING:

FORMING TECHNIQUE(S):

DECORATING TECHNIQUES & TOOLS:

DRYING TIME/NOTES:

BISQUE FIRING   DATE

KILN TYPE:	PROGRAM OR FIRING METHOD:	CONE:
PREHEAT/HOLD/COOL FIRING TIME/TEMP(S):		TOTAL TIME:
STAINS/SPRAYS/COMBUSTIBLES:		

Glaze(s)

BRAND:	COLOR/TRANSPARENCY/CHARACTERISTICS		
APPLICATION METHOD(S):		COATS/LAYER:	FOOD SAFE? **YES NO**

BRAND:	COLOR/TRANSPARENCY/CHARACTERISTICS		
APPLICATION METHOD(S):		COATS/LAYER:	FOOD SAFE? **YES NO**

BRAND:	COLOR/TRANSPARENCY/CHARACTERISTICS		
APPLICATION METHOD(S):		COATS/LAYER:	FOOD SAFE? **YES NO**

BRAND:	COLOR/TRANSPARENCY/CHARACTERISTICS		
APPLICATION METHOD(S):		COATS/LAYER:	FOOD SAFE? **YES NO**

BRAND:	COLOR/TRANSPARENCY/CHARACTERISTICS		
APPLICATION METHOD(S):		COATS/LAYER:	FOOD SAFE? **YES NO**

GLAZE FIRING 1   DATE

KILN TYPE:	PROGRAM OR FIRING METHOD:	CONE:
PREHEAT/HOLD/COOL FIRING TIME/TEMP(S):		TOTAL TIME:

GLAZE/LUSTER FIRING   DATE

KILN TYPE:	PROGRAM OR FIRING METHOD:	CONE:
PREHEAT/HOLD/COOL FIRING TIME/TEMP(S):		TOTAL TIME:

NOTES:

____

____

____

____

____

SALES RECORD

SALE LOCATION:	ESTIMATED VALUE/LISTING PRICE:	
SALE DATE:	TRANSACTION DETAILS:	FINAL PRICE:

PROJECT: DATE:

IMAGE or SKETCH

DIMENSIONS: WEIGHT:

CLAY

TYPE:	COLOR:	SOURCE:
ADDITIVE(S):		RESULTS RATING:

FORMING TECHNIQUE(S):

DECORATING TECHNIQUES & TOOLS:

DRYING TIME/NOTES:

BISQUE FIRING   DATE

KILN TYPE:	PROGRAM OR FIRING METHOD:	CONE:
PREHEAT/HOLD/COOL FIRING TIME/TEMP(S):		TOTAL TIME:
STAINS/SPRAYS/COMBUSTIBLES:		

Glaze(s)

BRAND:	COLOR/TRANSPARENCY/CHARACTERISTICS		
APPLICATION METHOD(S):		COATS/LAYER:	FOOD SAFE? **YES NO**

BRAND:	COLOR/TRANSPARENCY/CHARACTERISTICS		
APPLICATION METHOD(S):		COATS/LAYER:	FOOD SAFE? **YES NO**

BRAND:	COLOR/TRANSPARENCY/CHARACTERISTICS		
APPLICATION METHOD(S):		COATS/LAYER:	FOOD SAFE? **YES NO**

BRAND:	COLOR/TRANSPARENCY/CHARACTERISTICS		
APPLICATION METHOD(S):		COATS/LAYER:	FOOD SAFE? **YES NO**

BRAND:	COLOR/TRANSPARENCY/CHARACTERISTICS		
APPLICATION METHOD(S):		COATS/LAYER:	FOOD SAFE? **YES NO**

GLAZE FIRING 1   DATE

KILN TYPE:	PROGRAM OR FIRING METHOD:	CONE:
PREHEAT/HOLD/COOL FIRING TIME/TEMP(S):		TOTAL TIME:

GLAZE/LUSTER FIRING   DATE

KILN TYPE:	PROGRAM OR FIRING METHOD:	CONE:
PREHEAT/HOLD/COOL FIRING TIME/TEMP(S):		TOTAL TIME:

NOTES:

____

____

____

____

____

SALES RECORD

SALE LOCATION:		ESTIMATED VALUE/LISTING PRICE:
SALE DATE:	TRANSACTION DETAILS:	FINAL PRICE:

PROJECT: **DATE:**

IMAGE or SKETCH

DIMENSIONS: **WEIGHT:**

CLAY

TYPE:	COLOR:	SOURCE:
ADDITIVE(S):		RESULTS RATING:

FORMING TECHNIQUE(S):

DECORATING TECHNIQUES & TOOLS:

DRYING TIME/NOTES:

BISQUE FIRING   DATE

KILN TYPE:	PROGRAM OR FIRING METHOD:	CONE:
PREHEAT/HOLD/COOL FIRING TIME/TEMP(S):		TOTAL TIME:
STAINS/SPRAYS/COMBUSTIBLES:		

Glaze(s)

BRAND:	COLOR/TRANSPARENCY/CHARACTERISTICS		
APPLICATION METHOD(S):		COATS/LAYER:	FOOD SAFE? **YES NO**

BRAND:	COLOR/TRANSPARENCY/CHARACTERISTICS		
APPLICATION METHOD(S):		COATS/LAYER:	FOOD SAFE? **YES NO**

BRAND:	COLOR/TRANSPARENCY/CHARACTERISTICS		
APPLICATION METHOD(S):		COATS/LAYER:	FOOD SAFE? **YES NO**

BRAND:	COLOR/TRANSPARENCY/CHARACTERISTICS		
APPLICATION METHOD(S):		COATS/LAYER:	FOOD SAFE? **YES NO**

BRAND:	COLOR/TRANSPARENCY/CHARACTERISTICS		
APPLICATION METHOD(S):		COATS/LAYER:	FOOD SAFE? **YES NO**

GLAZE FIRING 1   DATE

KILN TYPE:	PROGRAM OR FIRING METHOD:	CONE:
PREHEAT/HOLD/COOL FIRING TIME/TEMP(S):		TOTAL TIME:

GLAZE/LUSTER FIRING   DATE

KILN TYPE:	PROGRAM OR FIRING METHOD:	CONE:
PREHEAT/HOLD/COOL FIRING TIME/TEMP(S):		TOTAL TIME:

NOTES:

____

____

____

____

SALES RECORD

SALE LOCATION:	ESTIMATED VALUE/LISTING PRICE:

SALE DATE:	TRANSACTION DETAILS:	FINAL PRICE:

PROJECT: **DATE:**

IMAGE or SKETCH

DIMENSIONS: WEIGHT:

CLAY

TYPE:	COLOR:	SOURCE:

ADDITIVE(S):	RESULTS RATING:

FORMING TECHNIQUE(S):

____

____

DECORATING TECHNIQUES & TOOLS:

____

____

DRYING TIME/NOTES:

____

BISQUE FIRING   DATE

KILN TYPE:	PROGRAM OR FIRING METHOD:	CONE:

PREHEAT/HOLD/COOL FIRING TIME/TEMP(S):	TOTAL TIME:

STAINS/SPRAYS/COMBUSTIBLES:

Glaze(s)

BRAND:	COLOR/TRANSPARENCY/CHARACTERISTICS		
APPLICATION METHOD(S):		COATS/LAYER:	FOOD SAFE? YES NO

BRAND:	COLOR/TRANSPARENCY/CHARACTERISTICS		
APPLICATION METHOD(S):		COATS/LAYER:	FOOD SAFE? YES NO

BRAND:	COLOR/TRANSPARENCY/CHARACTERISTICS		
APPLICATION METHOD(S):		COATS/LAYER:	FOOD SAFE? YES NO

BRAND:	COLOR/TRANSPARENCY/CHARACTERISTICS		
APPLICATION METHOD(S):		COATS/LAYER:	FOOD SAFE? YES NO

BRAND:	COLOR/TRANSPARENCY/CHARACTERISTICS		
APPLICATION METHOD(S):		COATS/LAYER:	FOOD SAFE? YES NO

GLAZE FIRING 1   DATE

KILN TYPE:	PROGRAM OR FIRING METHOD:	CONE:
PREHEAT/HOLD/COOL FIRING TIME/TEMP(S):		TOTAL TIME:

GLAZE/LUSTER FIRING   DATE

KILN TYPE:	PROGRAM OR FIRING METHOD:	CONE:
PREHEAT/HOLD/COOL FIRING TIME/TEMP(S):		TOTAL TIME:

NOTES:

____

____

____

____

____

SALES RECORD

SALE LOCATION:	ESTIMATED VALUE/LISTING PRICE:

SALE DATE:	TRANSACTION DETAILS:	FINAL PRICE:

PROJECT: **DATE:**

DIMENSIONS: WEIGHT:

CLAY

TYPE:		COLOR:	SOURCE:	
ADDITIVE(S):				RESULTS RATING:

FORMING TECHNIQUE(S):

DECORATING TECHNIQUES & TOOLS:

DRYING TIME/NOTES:

BISQUE FIRING   DATE

KILN TYPE:	PROGRAM OR FIRING METHOD:	CONE:
PREHEAT/HOLD/COOL FIRING TIME/TEMP(S):		TOTAL TIME:
STAINS/SPRAYS/COMBUSTIBLES:		

Glaze(s)

BRAND:	COLOR/TRANSPARENCY/CHARACTERISTICS		
APPLICATION METHOD(S):		COATS/LAYER:	FOOD SAFE? **YES NO**

BRAND:	COLOR/TRANSPARENCY/CHARACTERISTICS		
APPLICATION METHOD(S):		COATS/LAYER:	FOOD SAFE? **YES NO**

BRAND:	COLOR/TRANSPARENCY/CHARACTERISTICS		
APPLICATION METHOD(S):		COATS/LAYER:	FOOD SAFE? **YES NO**

BRAND:	COLOR/TRANSPARENCY/CHARACTERISTICS		
APPLICATION METHOD(S):		COATS/LAYER:	FOOD SAFE? **YES NO**

BRAND:	COLOR/TRANSPARENCY/CHARACTERISTICS		
APPLICATION METHOD(S):		COATS/LAYER:	FOOD SAFE? **YES NO**

GLAZE FIRING 1   DATE

KILN TYPE:	PROGRAM OR FIRING METHOD:	CONE:
PREHEAT/HOLD/COOL FIRING TIME/TEMP(S):		TOTAL TIME:

GLAZE/LUSTER FIRING   DATE

KILN TYPE:	PROGRAM OR FIRING METHOD:	CONE:
PREHEAT/HOLD/COOL FIRING TIME/TEMP(S):		TOTAL TIME:

NOTES:

____

____

____

____

____

SALES RECORD

SALE LOCATION:	ESTIMATED VALUE/LISTING PRICE:	
SALE DATE:	TRANSACTION DETAILS:	FINAL PRICE:

PROJECT: DATE:

IMAGE or SKETCH

DIMENSIONS: WEIGHT:

CLAY

TYPE:	COLOR:	SOURCE:
ADDITIVE(S):		RESULTS RATING:

FORMING TECHNIQUE(S):

DECORATING TECHNIQUES & TOOLS:

DRYING TIME/NOTES:

BISQUE FIRING   DATE

KILN TYPE:	PROGRAM OR FIRING METHOD:	CONE:
PREHEAT/HOLD/COOL FIRING TIME/TEMP(S):		TOTAL TIME:
STAINS/SPRAYS/COMBUSTIBLES:		

Glaze(s)

BRAND:	COLOR/TRANSPARENCY/CHARACTERISTICS		
APPLICATION METHOD(S):		COATS/LAYER:	FOOD SAFE? **YES NO**

BRAND:	COLOR/TRANSPARENCY/CHARACTERISTICS		
APPLICATION METHOD(S):		COATS/LAYER:	FOOD SAFE? **YES NO**

BRAND:	COLOR/TRANSPARENCY/CHARACTERISTICS		
APPLICATION METHOD(S):		COATS/LAYER:	FOOD SAFE? **YES NO**

BRAND:	COLOR/TRANSPARENCY/CHARACTERISTICS		
APPLICATION METHOD(S):		COATS/LAYER:	FOOD SAFE? **YES NO**

BRAND:	COLOR/TRANSPARENCY/CHARACTERISTICS		
APPLICATION METHOD(S):		COATS/LAYER:	FOOD SAFE? **YES NO**

GLAZE FIRING 1   DATE

KILN TYPE:	PROGRAM OR FIRING METHOD:	CONE:
PREHEAT/HOLD/COOL FIRING TIME/TEMP(S):		TOTAL TIME:

GLAZE/LUSTER FIRING   DATE

KILN TYPE:	PROGRAM OR FIRING METHOD:	CONE:
PREHEAT/HOLD/COOL FIRING TIME/TEMP(S):		TOTAL TIME:

NOTES:

____

____

____

____

____

SALES RECORD

SALE LOCATION:	ESTIMATED VALUE/LISTING PRICE:	
SALE DATE:	TRANSACTION DETAILS:	FINAL PRICE:

PROJECT: **DATE:**

DIMENSIONS: WEIGHT:

CLAY

TYPE:	COLOR:	SOURCE:
ADDITIVE(S):		RESULTS RATING:

FORMING TECHNIQUE(S):

DECORATING TECHNIQUES & TOOLS:

DRYING TIME/NOTES:

BISQUE FIRING   DATE

KILN TYPE:	PROGRAM OR FIRING METHOD:	CONE:
PREHEAT/HOLD/COOL FIRING TIME/TEMP(S):		TOTAL TIME:
STAINS/SPRAYS/COMBUSTIBLES:		

Glaze(s)

BRAND:	COLOR/TRANSPARENCY/CHARACTERISTICS		
APPLICATION METHOD(S):		COATS/LAYER:	FOOD SAFE? **YES NO**

BRAND:	COLOR/TRANSPARENCY/CHARACTERISTICS		
APPLICATION METHOD(S):		COATS/LAYER:	FOOD SAFE? **YES NO**

BRAND:	COLOR/TRANSPARENCY/CHARACTERISTICS		
APPLICATION METHOD(S):		COATS/LAYER:	FOOD SAFE? **YES NO**

BRAND:	COLOR/TRANSPARENCY/CHARACTERISTICS		
APPLICATION METHOD(S):		COATS/LAYER:	FOOD SAFE? **YES NO**

BRAND:	COLOR/TRANSPARENCY/CHARACTERISTICS		
APPLICATION METHOD(S):		COATS/LAYER:	FOOD SAFE? **YES NO**

GLAZE FIRING 1　　　　　　　　　　DATE

KILN TYPE:	PROGRAM OR FIRING METHOD:	CONE:
PREHEAT/HOLD/COOL FIRING TIME/TEMP(S):		TOTAL TIME:

GLAZE/LUSTER FIRING　　　　　　　　DATE

KILN TYPE:	PROGRAM OR FIRING METHOD:	CONE:
PREHEAT/HOLD/COOL FIRING TIME/TEMP(S):		TOTAL TIME:

NOTES:

____

____

____

____

____

SALES RECORD

SALE LOCATION:	ESTIMATED VALUE/LISTING PRICE:
SALE DATE:	TRANSACTION DETAILS:	FINAL PRICE:

PROJECT: **DATE:**

IMAGE or SKETCH

DIMENSIONS: WEIGHT:

CLAY

TYPE:	COLOR:	SOURCE:

ADDITIVE(S):	RESULTS RATING:

FORMING TECHNIQUE(S):

DECORATING TECHNIQUES & TOOLS:

DRYING TIME/NOTES:

BISQUE FIRING   DATE

KILN TYPE:	PROGRAM OR FIRING METHOD:	CONE:

PREHEAT/HOLD/COOL FIRING TIME/TEMP(S):	TOTAL TIME:

STAINS/SPRAYS/COMBUSTIBLES:

Glaze(s)

BRAND:	COLOR/TRANSPARENCY/CHARACTERISTICS		
APPLICATION METHOD(S):		COATS/LAYER:	FOOD SAFE? **YES NO**

BRAND:	COLOR/TRANSPARENCY/CHARACTERISTICS		
APPLICATION METHOD(S):		COATS/LAYER:	FOOD SAFE? **YES NO**

BRAND:	COLOR/TRANSPARENCY/CHARACTERISTICS		
APPLICATION METHOD(S):		COATS/LAYER:	FOOD SAFE? **YES NO**

BRAND:	COLOR/TRANSPARENCY/CHARACTERISTICS		
APPLICATION METHOD(S):		COATS/LAYER:	FOOD SAFE? **YES NO**

BRAND:	COLOR/TRANSPARENCY/CHARACTERISTICS		
APPLICATION METHOD(S):		COATS/LAYER:	FOOD SAFE? **YES NO**

GLAZE FIRING 1   DATE

KILN TYPE:	PROGRAM OR FIRING METHOD:	CONE:
PREHEAT/HOLD/COOL FIRING TIME/TEMP(S):		TOTAL TIME:

GLAZE/LUSTER FIRING   DATE

KILN TYPE:	PROGRAM OR FIRING METHOD:	CONE:
PREHEAT/HOLD/COOL FIRING TIME/TEMP(S):		TOTAL TIME:

NOTES:

____

____

____

____

SALES RECORD

SALE LOCATION:	ESTIMATED VALUE/LISTING PRICE:	
SALE DATE:	TRANSACTION DETAILS:	FINAL PRICE:

Notes

Notes

Notes

Notes

Notes

Notes